MW00612233

ENDORSEMENTS

This book just opened up a whole new realm of understanding to me!

The insight and revelation in *Kingdom Mysteries Hidden in Plain Sight* will allow the reader to finally see Jesus through new eyes. The truth of the crucifixion has been established from the beginning of time. As Adrian unfolds each chapter the clear understanding and Biblical reference to the finished work of Christ becomes even more apparent. This teaching will become a foundation for many in the Body of Christ who are looking to explore the depth of Christ's glorious kingdom.

LISA PERN
Touched by Prayer

Adrian leads us into fresh depths of interpretation of Scripture.

Adrian's book *Kingdom Mysteries Hidden in Plain Sight* is both revelatory and challenging. For those on a quest to discern and receive all the riches hidden in the Word of God, Adrian leads us into fresh depths of interpretation of Scripture, with the principles of the Kingdom firmly in view at all times. It is a revelatory journey, which simultaneously challenges us to set aside our assumptions about how Scripture speaks to us.

Adrian masterfully draws together seemingly disparate threads of scripture into a rich tapestry that constantly speaks of a deeper journey into the realm of the Spirit of God.

JOHN HEMANS
Senior Minister, Open Heaven Church
Sydney Australia

I have made this book a part of my daily devotional!

I love Adrian Beale. As I had the privilege of reading through *Kingdom Mysteries: Hidden in Plain Sight,* my heart was overjoyed as Adrian unlocked the deeper levels and mined golden truth that had been there in Scriptures I had read many, many times.

I love the Lord and His honor and gifts for those who diligently seek Him and dig deep into His eternal Word. He has rewarded Adrian richly and now Adrian is sharing the riches of the revelation in which he has been gifted with us.

I believe we are living in an hour when the Father is revealing the mysteries contained in His Word like never before. Adrian is one of the vessels who has proven himself a faithful miner of the true riches and is being used by the Father to deliver a payload of revelation and understanding to the Body of Christ.

JAMES NESBIT
Prophetic Art of James Nesbit
jnesbit.com

This book will help open the eyes of your heart.

Adrian Beale has a unique Holy Spirit-inspired ability to plumb the depths of Scripture and extract revelation that will stir you, stretch you, and build your faith. As you read *Kingdom Mysteries: Hidden in Plain Sight*, you will be empowered to live in the reality that the fullness of the kingdom is here and yours right now. You will shift from crying out for the kingdom to come, to realizing it has through Christ, and you will experience it manifesting in your life in a much, much greater way.

ROBERT HOTCHKIN
Founder, Men on the Frontlines/Patricia King Ministries
RobertHotchkin.com

A brilliant book!

Adrian's relationship with the Father, Son and Holy Spirit are evident in the pages of this book as he reflects the heartbeat of the Trinity in releasing truth into the hearts of the reader. The kingdom of God, a different spiritual dimension to the manifest world, is a kingdom accessible, tangible, and more relevant and real than most would ever perceive possible. This is the glorious kingdom we are now citizens and partakers of as the children of God.

Adrian takes time to unpack this revelation skillfully from Scripture, leaving the reader hungry for more. Our minds are a portal camped on the edge of two worlds, waiting to bring what we see in the kingdom through faith into this manifest place, earth.

Adrian is a true fivefold teacher and one of the most passionate people I know. He has skillfully laid out a pathway for all to find their way in his book *Kingdom Mysteries: Hidden in Plain Sight*. Thank you Adrian Beale for the person you are, for your courage to stand up and be counted. Debbie and I celebrate you.

GARY GRANT
Senior Spiritual Leader, Friends First Church, Melbourne, Australia
Director of Studies, Heart Academy, Melbourne, Australia

A rich well of revelation...

They say that true fivefold teachers spark revelation in their hearers. This is certainly true of our friend Adrian Beale and his latest book, *Kingdom Mysteries: Hidden in Plain Sight.*

This book is so full of remarkable insight that it births a desire in the reader to also mine the Scriptures for the treasures that they hold. Proverbs tells us, "It is the glory of God to conceal a matter and the glory of kings to search it out" (Prov. 25:2). As Adrian unpacks wonderful kingdom insights and intricate details hidden in the Word of God, we are compelled and equipped to want to continue the search for treasure in the Scripture. Thank you, Adrian, for this truly remarkable book!

KATHERINE RUONALA
Author of *Living in the Miraculous, Wilderness to Wonders,* and *Life with the Holy Spirit*
Senior Leader of Glory City Church Brisbane, Australia and GCN International
Founder and Facilitator of the Australian Prophetic Council

This wonderful book unveils profound mysteries.

We are living in an exciting time on earth, a time where God's kingdom has progressed from a mustard seed into the greatest tree in the garden. God's kingdom within us is ever increasing. His kingdom is the expression of our Father's heart for us and it is impregnated with His life and ability.

The only way God's people can freely enjoy the benefits of their rightful inheritance is through the understanding of how God's kingdom works in and through their lives. It is this transforming revelation revealed that is the power behind Adrian Beale's book, *Kingdom Mysteries: Hidden in Plain Sight.*

This wonderful book is layered with one profound example after another of God's kingdom, hidden for people who have eyes to see. As you read *Kingdom Mysteries: Hidden in Plain Sight,* I believe two things will happen. Firstly, you will be amazed at what Adrian unveils to you—profound mysteries lying just beneath the surface of familiar stories and Scriptures. Secondly, there will be a supernatural impartation of fresh hunger and anointing to receive your very own precious kingdom revelation.

I'm praying that you enjoy this incredible feast of life-giving revelation and everlasting kingdom truth as much as I have.

ANDREW MAGRATH
Pastor, Hope City Church, Melbourne, Australia

Adrian pulls apart Scripture in ways that I have never heard others do.

Adrian Beale is an amazing man of revelation. I remember spending time with him a couple of years ago, listening to him pull apart Scriptures. I cherished that about him. It is the same thing in this book. Over and over again he tackles Scriptures and shows us things that we never thought of before. I found myself thinking, *Yes, that is what that means....* In fact, just this week I had been thinking of the passage of Scripture where Jesus is walking with the disciples on the road to Emmaus. When I read what Adrian wrote, I understood that passage much better. You will thoroughly enjoy this read.

DR. DARREN CANNING
Almonte, Canada

In your hands is a treasure trove of revelation!

You are about step behind the veil to see Jesus Christ in a whole new light and receive revelation concerning God's kingdom and the Person in which all of heaven cries, "Holy." Adrian Beale's new book, *Kingdom Mysteries: Hidden in Plain Sight,* is a read that combines spiritual thoughts with spiritual words (1 Cor. 2:13). God has graced Adrian to beautifully put language to that which is in the unseen realm of the Scriptures. What I like about this book is that chapter by chapter there is a new invitation to partake and have fellowship with truth that is tangible.

I heartily endorse this book as I believe it will awaken fresh pursuit toward God in any person who reads.

ALEX PARKINSON
Mirror Image Ministries
Author of *Partakers of the Divine*

This is more than a book, it is a spiritual guide into the depths of the kingdom.

Once in a generation a person finds rare treasure mined deep in the heart of Yahweh. Adrian Beale is that kingdom miner, once again exquisitely presenting to us Jesus-centered, Holy Spirit-inspired teaching. In Matthew 13:44 the kingdom is attributed to that of a man finding treasure and selling everything to buy the field it was found in. *Kingdom Mysteries: Hidden in Plain Sight* shares that reality with the reader: the kingdom of Yahweh and His Christ is worth everything, and there is so much to explore.

With this new work Adrian continues to equip the saints and bring the Body of Christ up into maturity. *Kingdom Mysteries: Hidden in Plain Sight* is a treasure for the wider church and cuts across denominational divisions, opening up the expanse of Yahweh's kingdom, making it accessible for all believers. The truth contained within these pages has been carefully, biblically, and methodically composed, bringing to light insights that will empower, encourage, and equip believers. The revelation truth that has been scribed in these pages will enable generations of followers of Jesus to fully grasp, understand, apply, and live in the realities of the kingdom of God now and in the days to come. Steeped in rich and pure theological understanding, Adrian has been able to magnify the realities of the kingdom realm, whilst making the truth "plain" enough for all believers to grasp.

This book will be a forerunner for authors, poets, prophets, preachers, shepherds and everyone in between to "run" with the message of the kingdom and become ambassadors for Christ. Don't just read this book and move on. Take this kingdom field manual up on its offer and calling—slow down, rest and receive the kingdom truth that is and always has been "hidden in plain sight." See this deep and rich work as a kingdom map, creating a safe and biblical framework to explore, participate, and communicate the kingdom of God in an authentic and Christ-centered way.

ADAM and CATH OSBORNE
Founders of Sanctuary Australia, located in the Blue Mountains
www.sanctuaryaustralia.co

KINGDOM MYSTERIES

HIDDEN IN PLAIN SIGHT

DESTINY IMAGE BOOKS BY
ADRIAN BEALE AND ADAM F. THOMPSON

The Divinity Code

A Practical Guide to Decoding Your Dreams and Vision

God's Prophetic Symbolism in Everyday Life

DESTINY IMAGE BOOKS BY ADRIAN BEALE

The Mystic Awakening

KINGDOM MYSTERIES

HIDDEN IN PLAIN SIGHT

YOUR INVITATION TO ACCESS
AND RELEASE HEAVEN'S PROVISION

ADRIAN BEALE

© Copyright 2019–Adrian Beale

All rights reserved. This book is protected by the copyright laws of the United States of America. This book may not be copied or reprinted for commercial gain or profit. The use of short quotations or occasional page copying for personal or group study is permitted and encouraged. Permission will be granted upon request. Unless otherwise identified Scripture quotations are taken from the King James Version adjusted for modern readers by the author. This format simply utilizes the strength of the KJV as a literal translation and brings it into understandable English. Scripture quotations marked NKJV are taken from the New King James Version. Copyright © 1982 by Thomas Nelson, Inc. Used by permission. All rights reserved. All emphasis within Scripture quotations is the author's own. Please note that Destiny Image's publishing style capitalizes certain pronouns in Scripture that refer to the Father, Son, and Holy Spirit, and may differ from some publishers' styles. Take note that the name satan and related names are not capitalized. We choose not to acknowledge him, even to the point of violating grammatical rules.

DESTINY IMAGE® PUBLISHERS, INC.

P.O. Box 310, Shippensburg, PA 17257-0310

"Promoting Inspired Lives."

This book and all other Destiny Image and Destiny Image Fiction books are available at Christian bookstores and distributors worldwide.

Cover design by Eileen Rockwell
Interior design by Terry Clifton

For more information on foreign distributors, call 717-532-3040.

Reach us on the Internet: www.destinyimage.com.

ISBN 13 TP: 978-0-7684-5187-0
ISBN 13 eBook: 978-0-7684-5188-7
ISBN 13 HC: 978-0-7684-5190-0
ISBN 13 LP: 978-0-7684-5189-4

For Worldwide Distribution, Printed in the U.S.A.
1 2 3 4 5 6 7 8 / 23 22 21 20 19

CONTENTS

INTRODUCTION

My desire in writing this volume is to take the church beyond pure cliché references to the kingdom of heaven. So that, in growing in understanding of its existence and makeup, more believers would partake of its provision.

I do not wish to re-present what others are writing. The concepts presented here are, I believe, Holy-Spirit conceived. Stepping into new realms of the Spirit will mean that some of what is written will challenge current preconceived ideas. Therefore, be slow to reject something beyond your current understanding.

When the Spirit of God is speaking, it can be like a wheel within a wheel. This means, it may not be what is written in front of you that speaks to you, but rather what the Holy Spirit says to you through what you read. That is what you are to receive. What Scriptures, passages, relationships, and issues are brought to mind as you read?

This book will open the kingdom of heaven to you like never before. In doing so, it will provide answers to:

- Where is the kingdom?

- What is its landscape?

- What is its language?

- When is the kingdom coming into being?

- How do you enter the kingdom?

- Who may enter?

- What constitutes its glory?

- What is the significance that the kingdom is eternal?

If you like to be assured this is solid ground, what is presented is repeatedly backed with Scripture. Be aware that each reading is, on average, 1,200 words in length. That said, given these parameters, some discussions had to be "reined in" and only enough material presented to qualify the kingdom principles they cover. This allows further room for discussion and investigation by those so wired.

As you read, you will develop a new love for Scripture, a new love for Jesus Christ, and your heart will have a new foundation to see the manifestation of the promises of God.

Be blessed,
ADRIAN

Chapter 1

READY TO ENTER

The "Aha!" Moment

I once heard a missionary, who was about to be sent forth, say that he now realized that all he had done so far in his Christian life had been preparing for this moment. I similarly find myself in a place where I recognize that the previous books God has privileged me individually to pen, have all been to bring me to this point. What perhaps had been a disjointed series of revelatory insights now make absolute sense to me, as God has progressively revealed the bigger picture.

This book is the result of that understanding. My prayer is that I would do justice in presenting to you the glorious hidden kingdom of our Lord Jesus Christ as revealed through the history and stories found in the Old Testament and Gospels.

> *It is the glory of God to conceal a thing: but the glory of kings is to search it out* (Proverbs 25:2).

Beyond Types and Shadows

In the past, we thought that pictures of Christ in the Old Testament were "types and shadows" of an awaited New Testament event. However, while Israel's history is a time-phased series of events, you will discover the images of Jesus they reveal, hidden within the pages of the Bible, are not locked in time. Their discovery is like the sun's rays casting light through a window He has opened to us, catching facets of a multidimensional and eternal kingdom. So that, whenever the layers of a Bible narrative are peeled back to reveal Jesus, the glory of His kingdom is released.

Thus, when Jesus walked with two of His disciples on the Emmaus Road after His resurrection, we are told that their hearts burned within them as He opened the Scriptures about Himself to them. I would strongly suggest the fire they received was not the mere fluttering heartbeat of discovering a type or shadow, and it involved much more than Him opening Isaiah 53. It was, rather, a measure of the hidden glory of Christ's kingdom being released to them. There is a renewed interest in this passage of Scripture today because God is beckoning the church forward by drawing attention to the truth it contains.

The Need for Two Witnesses

It is critically important that as we press in more to see the glory of the kingdom manifest in healings, deliverances, and resurrections from the dead, that we also place beneath these outpourings a solid scriptural foundation. If we don't do this, we are in danger of continually losing the very ground we have gained. Like you, I want to experience more of His glory. It is wonderful to see healing and hear testimonies, but if it is only one subculture in the church experiencing the power of God, or if the same people are receiving prayer a year later for the same ailment, something is amiss.

Addressing this issue, we need to acknowledge that two key witnesses are required to confirm a word according to Scripture. I'm not talking about separate people testifying or making agreement in prayer, but rather, about individuals receiving confirmation within themselves, from both their head and heart. If people receive healing in the presence of God's glory without a corresponding scriptural understanding, then they are in jeopardy of having the evil one snatch the seed that was sown. When the head witnesses with what the heart is experiencing, then not only are more people open to receive, but the enemy has less leverage to steal the treasure that has been revealed.

Pastor Billy Graham

Many ministries have made comment about the passing of Pastor Billy Graham in February 2018. There is no question he was a remarkable salvation statesman of the Lord Jesus Christ, seeing thousands come to Christ through his crusades worldwide. While most weigh in on the significance of the event, by saying God is going to multiply Graham's work in crusades and mass salvation, I see it a little differently. Don't get me wrong, I believe there will be increased salvations worldwide. Like Billy, Moses was used by God to bring people out of Egypt—a picture of the world. However, with Moses passing, he released the baton to his replacement, Joshua, who brought Israel into the Promised Land. I see Graham's passing over, marked by a new breed rising, carrying fresh revelation to lead God's people into the Land of His Promises. Where Israel moved into the Promised Land, we have an inheritance known as the Land of His Promises.

It is no coincidence, that just as Israel had to leave a space of 2,000 cubits between themselves and the ark to enter Jordan, it has been 2,000 years since Christ entered eternity and we are now poised to follow on and "go by a way that we have not known before" (Joshua 3:4). The kingdom is no longer to be like an unfamiliar second cousin, but an heir, equal with redemption, following Christ's death upon the cross. The kingdom of heaven is our home to which we have all been granted access, that we may have opportunity to sink our teeth into its fruit.

This volume is designed so that you will come away with a firm hold on the kingdom of heaven—understanding its eternal nature, aware of its timing, familiar with its landscape, recognizing how to enter, and partaking of its glory.

Forty Days of Kingdom Preparation

Finally, this book is modeled on and inspired by Jesus' forty days teaching His disciples about the kingdom before He ascended to His throne (Acts 1:3; Hebrews 1:3). I have tried to avoid adding too much detail. Hence, each of the forty entries, drawn from familiar Bible passages, are deliberately succinct so that the kingdom truths they carry may be readily assimilated. Go slow and go low.

Application

In this section, you will find actions you can take, challenges, prayers, and some questions dependent on the material presented.

Israel moved into the Promised Land. What is it we move into?

Chapter 2

THE CROSS AND THE KINGDOM

Between Two Worlds

And he brought us out from there, that he might bring us in, to give us the land which he swore unto our fathers (Deuteronomy 6:23).

God brought them out, that He might bring them in. This is such a wonderful promise, and yet in hindsight, we know so many missed the boat. The children of Israel saw God's signs in Egypt and ate of His provision—manna and quail—along the way. They also sampled its giant-sized grapes, pomegranates, and figs firsthand as they awaited entry to their land flowing with milk and honey. Yet, unbelief led them to live out their days in the "no man's land" between two worlds. You could say, the giants of doubt and fear consumed them.

It's amazing that we can so often look at the Old Testament, and yet fail to see the importance of the parallel God has provided for our learning. Admittedly, some similarities are more obvious than others. Are we any different from the Israelites? Having come to the cross, we too have passed through the waters of baptism and have been positioned to have our minds set free from the dictates of this world. We have also tasted something of His goodness, provision, and even seen some miracles.

Nevertheless, like King David, in our hearts we know there is more, even this side of death (see Psalm 27:13).

In fact, there's so much more God wants us to enter into; but first, our minds have to be renewed to see it. The Israelites had first to daub their doors with the blood of the lamb before their journey could begin. We too have had the door of our hearts sprinkled with the blood of Lamb and been released from satan's clutches. In the chapter opening verse from Deuteronomy 6, that's the "brought us out" part. There is no "bringing us in" unless there has first been a bringing out. In other words, there is no kingdom unless there has first been a cross. The cross and the kingdom go hand in hand. Conversely, if you have come to the cross, the good news is the kingdom awaits.

The Cross and the Kingdom

Could our theology have so focused on the cross that it has blindsided us to the kingdom? Let me emphasize again—no cross, no kingdom. I'm not against the cross. God is eager to see people coming to the cross. In fact, as you will see, the cross is the door to the kingdom. You may be thinking, But Jesus is the door (John 10:9). Yes, Jesus is the door, but Jesus and the cross are synonymous. You cannot talk about Christ without thinking of the cross, and you cannot talk about the cross without thinking of Jesus. After all, He is the Eternal Lamb slain from the foundation of the world (Revelation 13:8).

However, if we camp at the cross, we are like people standing in the doorway never entering in to partake of the table of His provision. And if all we do is sing songs about His death and His blood and omit His majesty, glory, and goodness, we are subconsciously building walls of limitation in our hearts. In reinforcing just one side of the cross, we are also in danger of becoming a historical society without power and irrelevant to a dying world. God is about to bring so many more out, but He needs us to help them enter into their inheritance. Without the king-dom, all we have to offer is religious theology and programs, and God knows that wears thin very quickly.

In total accord with its Old Testament counterpart, and surpris-ingly divergent from much of what is taught today, the New Testament Scriptures reveal that there are two sides to Jesus' death upon the cross. Yes, there is redemption through His blood, but there is also an inher-itance found in the kingdom of the Son. That's the equivalent to our exodus from Egypt, and an entry into the Promised Land. In writing to the Colossians, the apostle Paul says:

> *Giving thanks unto the Father, which has privileged us to be partakers of the inheritance of the saints in light: Who has delivered us from the power of darkness, and has trans-lated us **into the kingdom** of his dear Son: In whom we have **redemption through his blood**, even the forgiveness of sins* (Colossians 1:12-14).

That's pretty straightforward, there's redemption through His blood and the kingdom. Here the apostle Paul shows their interdepen-dence by laying out first the kingdom and then redemption. Similarly, Jesus displayed this interdependent aspect when healing the man brought to Him on a stretcher. In perceiving the hearts of the scribes questioning His ability to forgive sins Jesus said:

> *For which is easier, to say, "Your sins be forgiven you"* [the cross]*; or to say, "Arise, and walk"* [the kingdom]*?* (Matthew 9:5)

Jesus cuts across all the religious red tape and shows the two—the cross and the kingdom—are coincident by simply demonstrating the glory of the kingdom. Similarly, we have the apostle Paul, before King

Agrippa, describing his mandate given by Christ Himself, reiterating the double-sided nature of the cross, when he says:

> *Delivering you...from the Gentiles, unto whom now I send you, To open their eyes, and to turn them from darkness to light, and from the power of Satan unto God, that they may receive* **forgiveness of sins,** *and* **an inheritance** *among them which are sanctified by faith that is in Me* (Acts 26:17-18).

Undergirding Christ's words to Paul are the cross and the kingdom, as seen in the "forgiveness of sins," and then, "an inheritance." It's pretty clear, the cross leads to the kingdom just as sure as leaving Egypt leads to the Promised Land.

Application

Jesus died to redeem us and open the kingdom of heaven to us. With which are you more familiar, the cross or the kingdom? Why?

In making a parallel journey with the Israelites, where would you honestly see yourself?

Are you in Egypt, coming through wilderness training, or taking ground in the kingdom?

Chapter 3

THE LANDSCAPE OF THE KINGDOM

Jesus only taught about the kingdom using parables for a number of reasons. One of those was because He was relating kingdom truth in language and imagery familiar to His hearers. In other words, He created scenes in the hearts of His listeners into which they could walk. There is a major truth here that is readily overlooked, the kingdom is entered through scenes framed and modeled in the mind and heart of believers.

In line with this Jesus said, *"The kingdom comes not with observation"* (Luke 17:20). He further went on to say, *"Neither shall they say, Lo here! Or, Lo there! For, behold, the kingdom of God is within you"* (Luke 17:21). This verse sets forth that we are portals to another realm. And as revolutionary as that thought may be, you are not only an access point through which the kingdom manifests on earth, your heart—thinking and imagination—is also the actual womb of the kingdom. By that I mean the human heart is the sphere from which the landscape of the kingdom emanates, flows, and issues forth. That means the shape or landscape of the kingdom is dependent on the nature of the way you and I think.

This is the reason why the majority of those who came out of Egypt were unable to enter their Promised Land. It is again the reason why two groups of people reading an identical passage in their Bibles, may perceive two very different messages—one of condemnation and the other of encouragement—dependent on their social conditioning. It is also why people who have faced or are facing environmental trauma are prone to regularly experience fearful dreams. In short, our heart disposition creates and shapes the parables that define our future.

Redefining Childlikeness

We have traditionally associated Jesus' call to be converted and become as little children, as a directive to be humbly dependent upon the authority of God, as His children, and that is a fair call. However, I find it very interesting that Jesus introduces this analogy of children in the lead up to a key teaching on the kingdom, where He does so using parables. Here He says:

> *Truly I say unto you, Except you be converted, and become as little children, you shall not enter into the kingdom of heaven* (Matthew 18:3).

A major difference between children and adults is the use of their imagination. As we mature, our Western system of schooling and training reinforces a reliance on logic and reason, rather than the ethereal world of one's imagination. And yet, think about it, all those who have excelled beyond their peers in their field of endeavor have been those who have harnessed the power of their imagination. It's true, people like Helen Keller, Albert Einstein, Nelson Mandela, Carl Sagan, Walt Disney, Marie Curie, Muhammed Ali, Lewis Carroll, William Blake, George Bernard Shaw, Oscar Wilde, and even Tony Robbins, to name but a few, all attribute their success to imagination and commitment.

Now, given that pride and humility are opposites, if we add to this observation our biblical understanding that it is "knowledge that puffs up" (1 Corinthians 8:1). It appears we have to acknowledge these imagination-rich individuals as really the ones who "humbled themselves as little children to become the greatest" (Matthew 18:4). Regardless of what you and I may think of them as individuals, we have to agree each of them broke through the ceiling of established knowledge to excel.

At this point, it is provocative that the root of two Hebrew words for "humble" are 1) *shach* (שָׁח) and 2) *anah* (עָנָה) and may be interpreted as: 1) the destroying of a wall, and 2) what comes from watching the inner life. In this context, this could suggest that when the wall of knowledge, that represents our pride, is knocked down and we "entertain" ourselves through active use of our imagination, we enter into a state of humility that is the ground for miracles.

How You Think Determines Your Experience

Jacob's name was changed to Israel, Saul became Paul, and Simon became Peter—and while these name changes were associated with a corresponding shift in character, the foundation and necessary forerunner to their transformation was a major transition in thinking. God had to change their thinking in order to position them to walk on a higher level to see His plans fulfilled. It is no coincidence, therefore, that we are similarly exhorted to have our minds, *renewed* to see the perfect will of God worked out in our lives (Romans 12:2).

Having a faith-filled mental attitude is not merely a good idea—the manifestation of the kingdom in our lives is dependent on it. In fact, there is not a more important factor in determining your kingdom experience than your thinking. Your prayer life and relationship with God are governed and limited by your mental disposition and heart attitude.

Little wonder the apostle Paul culminates his teaching to the Philippian church by writing:

> *Finally, brethren, whatsoever things are true, whatsoever things are honest, whatsoever things are just, whatsoever things are pure, whatsoever things are lovely, whatsoever things are of good report; if there be any virtue, and if there be any praise, think on these things* (Philippians 4:8).

Are there more defining Scriptures that open this further to us? I'm glad you asked, because from cover to cover, each Bible scene will add pegs for our imagination and fill the panorama of our understanding. Each verse or narrative provides more and more insight, so that we may lay claim to the land of our inheritance. That landscape and its glory is the thrust of this whole book.

Application

Take the time to imagine yourself in a parable scene that Jesus shared.

Would you say you are more or less imaginative than you were as a child?

If you have children, encourage them to exercise their imagination by getting them to picture scenes. Progressively, grow the scene and ask them what detail they see.

Today, practice catching negative thoughts before they germinate, affecting your attitude.

Chapter 4

THE GLORY OF THE KINGDOM

It is upon the landscape of our imagination that the kingdom reveals and tangibly manifests its glory. When Jesus turned water into wine at the wedding in Cana, it is recorded:

> *This beginning of miracles did Jesus in Cana of Galilee, and manifested forth his glory, and his disciples believed on him* (John 2:11).

This was a very significant event. This miracle was much more than an accelerated chemistry lesson. Take note here that Jesus' *"glory"* was not evident until He performed the miracle. John records it as Jesus' *beginning of miracles*, when technically, it wasn't the first miracle Jesus performed. Peter's conversion saw a miracle catch of fish which chronologically preceded this sign (Luke 5:5-8).

One of the reasons it is renown as *the beginning* is because of what it testifies. The turning of water to wine speaks beyond the awaited judgment associated with the turning of water to blood that was seen in Egypt (Exodus 7:14-21). It signals something far greater; it relays that through heaven's ultimate outpouring—Jesus' blood upon the cross—humankind will be filled with the joy of the Holy Spirit's presence. Therefore, it is noted as the manifestation of His glory, not so much because of the transsubstantiation miracle, at that moment, but because it forecasts the future infilling of believers at a wedding, a union, which would later become known as the outpouring on the Day of Pentecost. It foretold the end from the beginning.

Every Kingdom has an Associated Glory

Every kingdom has an associated glory. Nebuchadnezzar's kingdom had a glory (Isaiah 13:19; Daniel 2:37; 4:36; 5:18,20). Solomon's kingdom had a glory (Matthew 6:29). And the devil tested Jesus with the kingdoms of the world and their glory (Matthew 4:8). To aid our understanding of what constitutes His kingdom's glory, we can look at the commissioning of the disciples. Here, Jesus sent out the twelve to preach saying, *"The kingdom of heaven is at hand"* (Matthew 10:7). We are then shown its hidden glory when Jesus sends out the disciples to accompany the message they bore with signs and wonders. He commanded them not only to preach but also to heal the sick, cleanse lepers, raise the dead, and cast out demons (Matthew 10:8).

All miracles—contradictions of natural circumstances—are manifestations of His glory. Their foundation, or beginning as foretold in the turning of water to wine, is an endowment of power from the outpouring and indwelling of the Holy Spirit (Matthew 10:1; John 2; Acts 2).

John the Baptist

To fill out our understanding of the kingdom's glory, we can also look to the interaction between John the Baptist and Jesus. I'm talking about when John sent messengers to Jesus to question whether He was the awaited Messiah. That discourse was not a reasoned discussion but a demonstration of the glory of His kingdom. Each miracle was chosen to confirm that Jesus was Israel's Savior King. How were the signs Jesus performed confirmation that He was truly the One for whom John had been preparing Israel? Jesus' response to John was a fulfilling of the Law and the Prophets.

Now, when speaking about God's glory, our thoughts often lean toward Moses' encounter of the glory. On that occasion, when Moses asked to see God's glory (Exodus 33:18), we assume that Moses' encounter with the glory was the act of his being hidden in the cleft of the rock as God passed by him. However, before that happened, in response to Moses' request to see His glory, God said:

> *...I will make all my goodness pass before you, and I will proclaim the name of the Lord before you; and will be gracious* [a gracious act to someone in need] *to whom I will be gracious, and will show mercy* [deep sympathy and sorrow for someone afflicted accompanied with a desire to relieve the suffering] *on whom I will show mercy* (Exodus 33:19).

Following this, God then hid Moses and passed by revealing only His back to him. Why did God not reveal His face to Moses? May I suggest that God did not want His glory associated with an identity, but with His essence. The glory that passed by Moses was not merely an ultrabright light. The light actually contained the essence of God, His goodness, His mercy and grace.

So, in coming back to the messengers John sent to Jesus, Jesus fulfilled signs before them, foretold in chapters 35 and 61 of the Book of Isaiah, which culminate in the reinstatement and glorification of Zion among the nations. However, more importantly, what you can't see in this record of His ministry is that Jesus also displayed God's character in the process. Thus, we read in Matthew 11:2-5:

> *Now when John had heard in the prison the works of Christ, he sent two of his disciples, And said unto him, Are you he that should come, or do we look for another?*

17

Jesus answered and said unto them, Go and show John again those things which you do hear and see:

The blind receive their sight, (Isaiah 35:5)

and the lame walk, (Isaiah 35:6)

the lepers are cleansed, (Isaiah 61:1)

and the deaf hear, (Isaiah 35:5)

the dead are raised up, (Isaiah 61:1; hell a prison: Psalm 86:13; 89:48; Jonah 2:6)

and the poor have the gospel preached to them (Isaiah 61:1).

While John was expecting a physical kingdom with circumstances in his favor, the miracles and the essence of God that accompanied them, confirmed Jesus as Israel's long-awaited Messianic Prince.

If we consider that every king has a kingdom and that Jesus' kingdom is not of this world, we must also recognize that Jesus is revealing its glory. The glory of His kingdom is one of signs, wonders, and miracles. The interaction between John's messengers and Jesus also reveals that manifestations of glory come out of the overflow of God's heart for those in need. Hence, it is important that we are careful not to put the cart before the horse.

Kavod: Hand on the Inner House Door

One last insight on the glory comes from the Hebrew form of the word for "glory," is *kavod* (כָּבֹד), which is made up of three letters, *kaph, bet, dalet.* Together they spell out the phrase: hand on the inner house door. This word picture fits with our understanding that the kingdom of heaven is within us. Following from this discussion, we also recognize that the key that opens that door is the essence of God's mercy and grace.

Application

Following Jesus' testing in the wilderness, it is fair to say there are two kinds of glory. One is centered on material things, and the other on unseen things. Do you have any suggestions on how we can transition from treasure on earth to treasure in heaven?

Do you think sometimes we are prone to seek the manifestations apart from His goodness, mercy, and grace?

Chapter 5

A KINGDOM WHEN?

The Church Billboard

On my Instagram feed a while back, I noticed a photograph various people had posted and reposted of a church billboard, which read:

Faith is not hoping God can

It is knowing He will.

If the number of likes these posts received were a measure of the agreement and endorsement they received, then many people believe the statement to be correct. However, I believe the statement as cited is incorrect. For me, to have so many followers agreeing with this statement of faith is indicative, potentially, of an underlying wrong belief system. I believe the post should instead read:

Faith is not hoping God can

It is knowing He has.

Do you see the difference? Both lines of the posting in its first form await a future fulfillment. That is not faith but is rather a statement of hope. Hope is a confident future expectation. Whereas faith is recognition that you now possess what was hoped for. It is a confidence that once God releases a word of revelation, you have what was promised.

While those who agreed with the first statement are likely giving assent to the thought that God will do what He promised—an absolute truth—the problem arises when this is diluted to become, "God will someday do what He promised." It is the open-ended nature of this confession that is the issue, because such a belief opens the door to doubt as people wait, endlessly hoping that someday they will receive the promise.

In relation to the subject of this book, the point is that if the kingdom is just some future-awaited event, then there is likely to be a lot of disillusioned believers not walking in the victory and substance of what they had hoped for. Those who are always leaving but never arriving, and always sowing but not seeing a return. On this point Scripture warns, *"Hope deferred makes the heart sick"* (Proverbs 13:12). As disillusionment readily leads to disgruntlement, which in turn may lead to disengagement, this wrongly held belief could be a contributing factor for the many once on-fire believers living independent of the church today.

The Kingdom's Timing

Therefore, it is important to settle in our hearts the timing of the establishment of the kingdom of God. While there are Scriptures that appear to project a future kingdom, there are equally as many that declare the kingdom is in place right now. This is where an understanding of the eternal nature of the kingdom accommodates the truth that the kingdom is both here now and in the future.

How do we know the kingdom is here now? Let's first acknowledge the miracles that are currently taking place through multitudes of ministries worldwide. Like those Jesus presented to John the Baptist, miracles are His kingdom ambassador's official seal. For those who also like a scriptural grounding, a number of verses will settle the issue. The prophet Isaiah associated the establishment of the kingdom, with a child called, *"Wonderful, Counsellor, the mighty God, the everlasting Father, the Prince of Peace"* (Isaiah 9:6). He also went on to describe for us its timing, longevity, and expansion when he said:

> *Of the increase of his government and peace there shall be no end, upon the throne of David, and upon his kingdom, to order it, and to establish it with judgment and with justice from henceforth even forever...* (Isaiah 9:7).

Like Jesus' disciples (Acts 1:6), our propensity as we read this, because of its mention of David's throne, is to look for the establishment of a formal State. Yet, Jesus declared to Pilate, *"My kingdom is not of this world..."* (John 18:36). So while we await a future physical dispensation, we might consider that these verses link the revelation to the hearts of men and women of Christ's deity, with the establishment of His kingdom. What's more, once in place, it is to continually increase without interruption forever. Both the King's identity and continuous reign was confirmed by the angel that visited Mary, who explained the Babe she was about to birth would *"reign over the house of Jacob, and of His kingdom there would be no end"* (Luke 1:33).

Its continual increase without any break is in contrast to those who purport that the power of the outpouring recorded in the Book of Acts died with the apostles. Not only did Jesus say that all authority had been given to Him (Matthew 28:18), but He also spent forty days instructing the disciples on the kingdom before ascending to His heavenly throne (Acts 1:3). Think about it, this latter act makes very little sense unless the disciples were about to step into it. The writer to the Hebrews again reiterates for us the sequence of events that disclose its timing; when speaking of the Son, he writes:

Who being the brightness of his glory, and the express image of his person, and upholding all things by the word of his power, when he had by himself purged our sins, sat down on the right hand of the Majesty on high (Hebrews 1:3).

So after Jesus had redeemed us through His blood, His kingdom was established as signified by sitting down on His heavenly throne. In Paul's letter to the Ephesians he adds:

...When he ascended up on high, he led captivity captive, and gave gifts unto men (Ephesians 4:8).

This is the depiction of a victory parade for a triumphant king returning to his throne from the field of battle, freeing and bringing with him those held by the enemy and returning the spoils of war to his people. This means that John the Baptist, not only was a herald of Christ's arrival, he also broadcast the arrival of God's kingdom, when he declared the kingdom was *"at hand"* (Matthew 3:2). This all makes sense and fits with the words of Christ when He says that some standing before Him would not taste death *"until they saw the Son of man coming in His kingdom"* (Matthew 16:28). Though unseen, the kingdom has nonetheless been in operation since its inception through Christ's death, resurrection, and ascension, and is in operation right now.

The Gospel of the Kingdom

In Matthew's account of Christ's ministry, he makes deliberate reference three times to the phrase, *"the gospel of the kingdom"*:

And Jesus went about all Galilee, teaching in their synagogues, and preaching the gospel of the kingdom, and healing all manner of sickness and all manner of disease among the people (Matthew 4:23).

And Jesus went about all the cities and villages, teaching in their synagogues, and preaching the gospel of the kingdom, and healing every sickness and every disease among the people (Matthew 9:35).

And this gospel of the kingdom shall be preached in all the world for a witness unto all nations; and then shall the end come (Matthew 24:14).

You will notice that the first two recorded incidents of the term's use have with them not only preaching and teaching, but more importantly the demonstration of the kingdom with its associated healing of all types of sickness and disease. Notice also that on the final occasion Jesus says this gospel of the kingdom will be preached as *"a witness."* What do you think was the witness in the first two verses? The answer, of course, was the healing of all manner of sickness and disease.

Why does the final verse not mention healing? Its absence in context of His summary of end-time signs is not a denial of power today. On the contrary, it is a confirmation that His followers will move with demonstrated power, no matter where they are on the globe. Otherwise, it would not be an equally true witness of the kingdom.

Application

Why is it important to recognize the kingdom is here now? (See Matthew 8:13; 9:29; 15:28.)

If you are honest, would you say your Christian walk exemplifies someone who sees the kingdom as present or future?

Do you know people, who once walked with God, but have returned into the world because they became disillusioned with waiting?

Jesus is still in the business of distributing gifts taken from satan's strongholds. Do you know the gifts and talents your family has lost, that are your rightful inheritance? Ask Jesus for them today.

Chapter 6

ENTRY THROUGH REVELATION

Recognizing the two-fold nature of the gospel—cross and kingdom—after briefly glimpsing the landscape and having our expectations whetted by its present operation, we now turn to consider how entry is gained on a personal level.

Understanding the parallel of Israel's path through the wilderness with our own journey to the Land of God's Promises provides key insights into our quest to enter the kingdom. One verse in particular stands out starkly as the pivotal lesson the children of Israel were to learn in the wilderness before they could go forward. This is such an important lesson we need to pay close attention:

> *And he humbled you, and suffered you to hunger, and fed you with manna, which you knew not, neither did your fathers know; that he might make you know that man does not live by bread only, but by every word that proceeds out of the mouth of the Lord does man live* (Deuteronomy 8:3).

In summarizing Israel's sojourn in the wilderness to the next generation, why is this dependence on manna such a critical factor? And why would God want to teach Israel and the generations to follow this lesson? Looking at this verse in Deuteronomy 8, it is important to recognize that the life-giving manna is a metaphor for the word that *proceeds* from God's mouth. This means that manna is a parallel of the *rhema* or spoken word of revelation. It is here we discover that the transition through the wilderness was to build within Israel a humble heart to look for manna every day. Now, because of the parallel of manna and revelation, this experience was to establish within them a dependence on revelation as they went forward.

First up, the inclusion of past and present generations in not knowing manna suggests that each successive age needs to recognize its own vital need of revelation. Acknowledging that both current and past generations had never known manna says that this was more than just something new. If it was merely the introduction of something new, it would have been sufficient only to say that past generations hadn't known it. Of that generation that died in the wilderness, the wisdom of hindsight tells us that they had a slave mentality that had them seeing themselves as *"grasshoppers"* in their own sight (Numbers 13:33).

The inclusion of the current generation, those not conditioned by Egypt, suggests that this dependence on revelation provided more than a mere change to a limited mindset based on past experience. It presented both deliverance from the past limitation and an equal challenge to the present, the status quo.

Therefore, this verse holds such importance because in outlining Israel's daily dependence on manna, it reflects on us to recognize that revelation:

1. Is God's vehicle to challenge limited thinking,

and

2. Is able to provoke our complacency over an existing condition, by providing the means to frame up something beyond ourselves so that we can possess the future before it tangibly manifests.

As the daily search for manna was each Israelite's responsibility, it speaks to us of our individual need to seek for revelation. Do we see this need for manna reflected anywhere in the New Testament? Well, in outlining how we are to pray, Jesus said:

> *Thy kingdom come. Thy will be done in earth, as it is in heaven. Give us this day our daily bread* (Matthew 6:10-11).

What is daily bread? It's manna. This is not as has been taught, a request for the means to earn our daily provision. Once we understand manna is revelation, it couldn't be more direct. This is a call and expectation, that our prayer will release revelation from heaven so that the kingdom may manifest here on earth.

The Sole of Your Foot

When God was instructing Joshua prior to entry into the Promised Land, He said, *"Every place that the sole of your foot shall tread upon I have given you"* (Joshua 1:3). At one level, Israel's people were assured that they would take possession of every acre of land into which they initiated a takeover. On a totally different plane, it holds a much deeper truth. The word "sole" used here is the Hebrew word *kaph,* which, among other things, is also employed to describe a concave form such as a cupped hand, spoon, or vessel.

Therefore, it also describes the human heart, which, as a concave vessel, is capable of *"overflowing," "being filled"* and *"poured out"* (Psalm 23:5; Acts 2:4; Lamentations 2:19). This means the instruction to Joshua, on the eve of entry, also has within it the hidden truth that when God releases a spoken word or revelation to our heart, it becomes the ground on which we can put our weight in order to step in and possess the kingdom. By way of example, when Peter stepped out of the boat, he was not so much walking on water, but upon the word spoken by Jesus to *"Come"* (Matthew 14:28-29).

Meditation: The Ground on which Revelation Is Sown

Of course, the centerpiece of God's instruction to Joshua was the importance of meditation day and night in the Law. Therefore, following Moses' summation of the wilderness lessons comes a call to meditate on God's Word because meditation is the ground on which revelation is sown. God said to Joshua:

> *This Book of the Law shall not depart out of your mouth; but you shall meditate therein day and night, that you may observe to do according to all that is written therein: for then you shall make your way **prosperous,** and then you shall have good **success** (Joshua 1:8).*

While the words *"prosperous"* and *"success"* used here are in danger of becoming clichés today, their Hebrew counterparts are very insightful. The Hebrew word for "prosperous" is *salah,* and is elsewhere translated as a rushing or breaking forth, which, when you think about it, is exactly what revelation is—a breaking forth of insight from another realm. Complementing this is the Hebrew word for "success," *sakal,* which also describes prudent understanding. Thus, meditation in God's Word promises revelation and the wisdom to know what to do with it.

Application

What has been your latest revelation?

How does revelation deal with past mindsets and at the same time take us forward?

Chapter 7

BRINGING ETERNITY INTO TODAY

Early in Matthew's record of Jesus' ministry, there is an account where He healed Peter's mother-in-law of a fever, and that evening they brought Him many who were demon-possessed. At the time, He cast the demons out with a word and healed all those who were sick. You are likely familiar with the story; if not, it is found in Matthew 8:14-16. What you may not have noticed, however, is the verse that follows, where it says that He performed this ministry:

> *That it might be fulfilled which was spoken by Isaiah the prophet, saying, Himself took our infirmities, and bore our sicknesses* (Matthew 8:17).

May I ask you a question? When did Jesus bear our sickness and take our infirmities? The answer, according to Isaiah, was during His passion: from the whipping post to the cross (Isaiah 53:4-5). If that is the case, then He was ministering in the completed work of the cross, before the cross. Stop and think about that for a moment. Jesus was ministering outside of chronological time. At this point, He had not physically been to the cross, and yet He accessed its provision. He was operating from the eternal realm and bringing it into this realm. You

31

could say He stepped outside of the restraints of chronological time and brought eternal provision into today.

Healed by a Word Given Two Years Earlier

By way of example in accessing eternal promises, let me share a story. When Adam F. Thompson and I were being interviewed by Sid Roth for his program *It's Supernatural!,* we had the pleasure of meeting Smith Wigglesworth's great-granddaughter, Lil De Fin. Lil is a firebrand for Jesus and was also in the studio to record a program. During our short time together, one of the things she related was that she had been healed of malaria through a word of knowledge given by Pat Robinson on CBN, the Christian television network he founded. The only thing was that Pat had given the word two years prior to Lil hearing it and receiving its provision. Lil's healing demonstrates the eternal nature of the kingdom. She was healed by receiving a word given outside her time zone.

The Eternal Cross

While we are discussing the cross, would it be okay for me to ask you one more question? When did the cross take place? We are inclined to think and say AD 33. However, the last book of the Bible, the Book of Revelation, says Jesus is *"the Lamb slain from the foundation of the world"* (Revelation 13:8), which means, in eternal terms, it had taken place from time immemorial. Therefore, the cross was a reality outside of this realm long before Roman soldiers nailed Jesus to that tree.

Revelation 13:8 also tells us both Jesus and the cross existed from the very beginning, and through the hallways of time from the genesis of life on earth till its close, it has always been there. This is truly a remarkable and wondrous thing. This means that outside the demands of earth's agenda and heaven's provision, the peace of the cross has also always been there. When Jesus ministered, He was living and operating from that place, outside of earth's convulsions. So, whether it was the aspirations of the Roman Empire back then or our personal struggles today, heaven is there in the background awaiting all who understand and know how to access its provision.

Indeed, Jesus made reference to a spiritual reality beyond our own when He said to Pilate, *"My kingdom is not of this world"* (John 18:36). And without digressing, it should be noted that ultimately He was alluding to the victory of the cross when He gave thanks and He broke bread to feed 5,000-plus men, women, and children. And again, when He made reference to seeing Abraham, who rejoiced to see His day (John 8:56), He was saying they had met in that eternal realm. What's more, Abraham understood the ramifications of Jesus' sacrifice because he rejoiced.

If we consider creation to be the birthplace of physical life on earth, then in preceding time, like Christ, the cross has to be at the center of history because of its eternal span and influence. The cross is God's glorious masterstroke, for in it, there is provision to turn every negative situation into a blessing. All of God's favor and provision is released through the application of the cross and *every* Bible blessing is fulfilled, accessed, and realized through the cross.

The Fullness of Time

Therefore, in light of our discussion on gaining an eternal perspective, there is a double play at work in the verse that says, *"But when the fullness of time had come God sent His Son"* (Galatians 4:4). Though we primarily read this from an earthly standpoint as a reference to reaching a chronological marker on a timeline, it also rings true in relating to eternity. According to Hugh Ross, PhD, in *Beyond the Cosmos,* "Eternity is not merely outside chronological time, or timeless. It is rather, the fullness of time."[1] Everything that has ever taken place or is yet to take place is in the eternal realm. Many people think of eternity as timeless, but doing so puts it in a realm beyond cause and effect, and that contradicts what the Bible teaches.

From an eternal perspective, this verse from the Book of Galatians can be interpreted as God sent His Son so that we could partake of heaven's fullness. Just as Jesus stepped in and out of eternity beyond the chronological timeline to pre-access heaven's provision, we likewise are privileged as sons and daughters to partake of every victory, blessing, and promise documented in Scripture. We are able to do this because the cross is the ultimate focus, culmination, and true fulfillment of every Bible blessing.

This means that when we identify the cross and its ancillary events in the Old Testament, we are not merely unearthing a type and shadow of a future event. We are, in fact, accessing dimensions of the victory of the cross, unable to be documented in the one-dimensional Gospel accounts of Christ's physical sacrifice.

Jubilee

This book looks at many Old Testament and Gospel Scriptures to unfold the provision they hold for us today. A brief example here should suffice to demonstrate this truth. The Year of Jubilee (Leviticus 25:8-11) is when, if you had lost your inheritance, your ancestral land and home, you would receive back what was forfeited. As an Israelite, if you had fallen on hard times and been forced into servitude as a slave, at Jubilee you would be freed to return to your ancestral possession. Also, at the sound of the shofar proclaiming the Year of Jubilee, all debts would be cancelled. Finally, Jubilee, as a Sabbatical year, meant that the soil and the people were to rest.

The Year of Jubilee commenced on one very significant day, Yom Kippur, the Day of Atonement. The blessings of Jubilee could only follow after the Day of Atonement. What is the ultimate atonement? Jesus' sacrifice upon the cross. This means that in the cross there is Jubilee provision. The cross is the eternal and ultimate door to Jubilee; and therefore, as a spiritual Israelite, you now have access to your spiritual inheritance. You are no longer a slave to sin, all spiritual debts against your name are cancelled, and you are no longer working toward right-standing with God—you can rest in the completed work of Christ.

Application

Pause and meditate for a moment on the fact that Jesus ministered the provision of the cross before it had chronologically taken place.

What does it mean that every Bible blessing is fulfilled, accessed, and realized through the cross?

ENDNOTE

1. Hugh Ross, *Beyond the Cosmos: What Recent Discoveries in Astrophysics Reveal about the Glory and Love of God* (Kissimmee, FL: Signalman Publishing, 2010).

Chapter 8

I SAW SATAN FALL
LIKE LIGHTNING

A Fresh Look at a Familiar Verse

It is really easy to miss the deeper truth behind a verse of Scripture because at first glance its meaning or fulfillment appears obvious. One such familiar verse where an Old Testament word and its Gospel fulfillment appears to be pretty much tied down is found in chapter 53 of the Book of Isaiah:

> *And he made his grave with the wicked, and with the rich in his death; because he had done no violence, neither was any deceit in his mouth* (Isaiah 53:9).

In light of our understanding of the kingdom of God being present and in operation now, this verse has head-turning relevance for us today. We have always held that *"the wicked"* are the robbers with whom Jesus was crucified, and that *"the rich"* was a reference to Joseph of Arimathea. Look up any Bible cross-reference tool for Isaiah 53:9 and you will be taken to these two incidents. That said, the second part of the verse is interpreted for us by the apostle Peter when he quotes it, saying, *"Who committed no sin, Nor was deceit found in His mouth"* (1 Peter 2:22 NKJV).

Therefore, inserting Peter's understanding of the second part of the verse, back in the original prophecy, we read:

> *And he made his grave with the wicked, and with the rich in his death; because He did no sin, Nor was deceit found in his mouth* (Isaiah 53:9).

This means Jesus' sinless life secured for Him a death with the wicked and a rich man's sepulchre, once He had died. Hang on. Think about it. That's like saying, living a sinless life bought Jesus a miserable death, but a nice coffin. How does that seem appropriate?

Digging a little deeper we find that one of the meanings for the word "grave" is the Hebrew word *qeber* and is indeed grave, but it also means the end of life, in contrast to the womb. Similarly, the word "death" is the Hebrew word *mawet* and does mean death; it also means the place where the dead dwell. Now the verse seems to be opening up to make more sense so that the verse would now read something like this: And Jesus made the end of His life with the wicked, and afterward with the rich, because He did no sin, neither was guile found in His mouth.

This seems to suggest there are two scenes being played out here. The first records the cessation of physical life, while the other depicts what takes place beyond the veil of this world. One records what took place physically, and the other what took place spiritually. Though Jesus died among sinners, He moved into glory once departed. Now the consequence seems to fit with Christ's sinlessness, as recorded by Peter.

The only thing is, however, the word "death" in the original Hebrew is plural. So, the original verse actually says:

And he made his grave with the wicked, and with the rich in his deaths; because he had done no violence, neither was any deceit in his mouth (Isaiah 53:9).

Every Blow Brought Him Greater Glory

This is where things get really interesting. Most commentators say that the plural used in the word "deaths" here depicts an intensity and violence applied to the Suffering Servant's death. While the Gospel accounts seem to endorse this interpretation, here's the interesting part, the word "deaths," (death, plural) is only used here and in one other particular passage. A passage that just happens to be a proclamation against the king of Tyre, that is, wait for it, also openly recognized as a prophetic judgment against satan (see Ezekiel 28:2-19; especially verses 8 and 10).

So, while there appears to be an apparent surface fulfillment of this prophecy from the Old Testament, there is actually a much deeper story at play. Due to its precise use, only twice, it appears that the compounding deaths, experienced by both sides, would suggest that every blow against Christ brought Him greater glory, and at the same time struck at the devil.

Adding weight to this thought is the literal translation of God's warning to Adam in the garden about eating of the fruit of the knowledge of good and evil. While our Bibles record that He said, *"in the day you eat of it you shall surely die"* (Genesis 2:17), the literal translation says, *"in the day you eat of it in dying you shall die."* It appears God was talking about a progressive or multilayered death here. At this point, we need to recognize two things. First, Jesus Christ, as the Last Adam, similarly went through a multidimensional death. Second, under the law, judgment was metered according to the crime—an eye for an eye, a tooth for a tooth, etc.

Whoever sinned according to the law was to receive a penalty commensurate with the crime. However, within the law, any person bringing false witness was subject to the same judgment wished upon the innocent party (Deuteronomy 19:16,18-19). God's masterstroke is presented in the composite picture painted by Scripture. Not only did Christ make a parallel multidimensional downward journey with that of Adam, He also set forth the multilayered judgment upon satan as Christ's false accuser and the instigator of the fall. Truly, through the victory of the cross, satan was about to find out why it would be better that a millstone be tied around his neck in tampering with human-kind's innocence (Matthew 18:6).

This is why when Jesus greeted the seventy who marvelled at demons being subject to them in His name, He said, *"I saw Satan fall like lightning from heaven"* (Luke 10:18). Therefore, following from an understanding that eternity is the fullness of time, may I also put forward that every Old Testament account of Jesus' passion, as a multi-dimensional event, sets forth riches for us to partake, which when apprehended strike a blow at the heart of satan. Identifying the particular facet each Old Testament interdimensional account sets forth puts substance to the riches, which we, in Christ, are now able to partake.

Application

How does, the following verse from the Book of Romans, sit with what has been unlocked here?

And we know that all things work together for good to them that love God, to them who are the called according to his purpose (Romans 8:28).

Chapter 9

THE EMMAUS ROAD

Luke 24:13-35

I remember a number of years ago, as a Bible college student, when my classmate, Barry, delivered his message entitled, "What Things?" He was speaking on Jesus' discussion with the two dejected disciples making their way from Jerusalem on the Emmaus Road. His title was one that stuck in my mind, and the passage he chose holds a good deal of intrigue for all of us.

First, the King James Bible says that the disciple's eyes were *"holden,"* that they did not know Him. "Holden" means that their eyes were held fast, grasped, or held back from understanding who He was. Was that veiling something of their own making, or was it a divine act? It appears the ball was primarily in their court because Jesus referred to them as being *"slow of heart to believe,"* and even after having the Scriptures opened, as their hearts burned within them, they still did not know Him. It was only after He broke bread with them that they knew who He was.

I believe this was a case of their lack of expectancy, limiting God. Their projection of the future did not include Jesus passing through death to enter His glory, and therefore His promise of rising on the third day, nor the writings of the prophets found a place of belief in their hearts. What about us? What if we don't realize the kingdom is here today? A limited outlook and negative confession puts a restraint on God who is always waiting for people to exercise faith in His promises, to manifest the kingdom.

There was a critical juncture on this journey where the plot could have gone either way. This was when the party of travelers came near to the place where they were going to stay overnight. Here, Luke records that Jesus *"made as though He would have gone further."* Say what? You mean He would have moved on, had He not received an invitation to come in? I would have thought He was bursting with things to tell them. Especially after the victory of the resurrection; but no, Jesus was prepared to pass them by had they not invited Him in to commune with them.

What do we learn from Jesus awaiting an invitation before being revealed over the breaking of bread? Is it not that way post-ascension as well? He awaits an invitation to join us, that we also might enter into an experiential knowledge of Him as we taste and see His provision.

Jesus Is Revealed in the Breaking of Bread

Then, having successfully navigated that test, and it appeared His presence was secure inside, as they broke bread together, the duo recognized Him, and just like that, He was gone. I should point out the Bible doesn't actually say, they "recognized" Him, it says, *"their eyes were opened, and they knew Him"* at which point He vanished out of their sight.

Do you think it was the way He broke the bread, or what was conveyed in the breaking of it that opened their understanding? You see, I don't believe it was just a case of Him waiting for the penny to drop before leaving. What I'm asking is, was it a trigger or a marker? In documenting the event, Luke says Jesus took bread, blessed, broke, and gave it to the disciples. Why was it that He disappeared after this step-by-step process? If it was the process or His technique in breaking bread that pegged it for them, then His actions were a trigger. However, in leading them to the table before leaving, Jesus forever linked His revealing with the breaking of bread, and the event has to be a marker. Though His manner may have triggered their enlightenment, His disappearance at their discovery at the breaking of bread most certainly means they had come to the crux of the lesson. That is, Jesus is revealed in the breaking of bread.

This post-resurrection encounter warrants our attention because just as the disciples were blind to His presence and victory, we are similarly veiled to His kingdom and its provision. The good news is that there is a spiritual parallel in Jesus opening the Scriptures and His revealing in the breaking of bread that opens His kingdom to us today.

Communion

Jesus called us to partake of communion in *"remembrance"* of Him:

> *And he took bread, and gave thanks, and broke it, and gave unto them, saying, This is my body which is given for you: this do **in remembrance** of me* (Luke 22:19).

Though this particular verse is written in Greek, its counterpart in Hebrew is *zakar* or remember, to which Jesus is making reference, has a three-fold meaning. It means: 1) a memorial or sign; 2) to think on, to recall, or call to mind; and finally, 3) to invoke, mention or make known. Taking communion is not meant to be a repetitive and empty ritual. There is no denying, it is first a sign or memorial of the cost. However, that is only half the story. We, like the two disciples traveling to Emmaus, are prone to miss that Jesus passed through death to enter

His glory, *"Ought not Christ to have suffered these things, and to enter into his glory?"* (Luke 24:26). And the Bible says Jesus endured the cross for the joy set before Him (Hebrews 12:2). It also says He became poor, that we through His poverty might become rich (2 Corinthians 8:9).

Thus, it should come as no surprise that the Hebrew word pictures that make up the word "remember" reinforces this aspect of the breaking of bread as a unilateral, one-sided covenant meal. The Hebrew word *zakar* is made of three letters: (זָכַר) *zayin, kaph, reysh*:

Zayin: ז Weapon, cut

Kaph: כַ Cupped hand

Reysh: ר Head, person

With this insight, the three letters in context spell out: cut the hand of a person. This is a picture of covenant cutting between two parties (Isaiah 49:15-16). Our covenant with God is similar to what existed between David and Jonathan, where, as the king's son, Jonathan was the provider, and David was the receiver of the benefits of that covenant.

Therefore, from this foundation, the breaking of bread is meant to bring focus to the multifaceted provision that we have the privilege to declare into being. That's right, the bread of which we partake, symbolizing His broken body, is not just the morbid one-dimensional tearing of His flesh. It is also the opening up of the multidimensional bread of heaven, with all of its provision.

Where is that provision? Well, Jesus deliberately used the encounter on the Emmaus Road to link the disciples' burning hearts of revelation, as He opened the Scriptures about Himself with the breaking of bread. What this means is, uncovering Jesus in the Old Testament is not merely a type or shadow of things to come. No, the discovery of Christ in the Law and the Prophets opens facets of His victory at the cross that are otherwise hidden from the natural human.

The Gospel accounts of Jesus' passion capture the cost of our redemption, but the hidden Old Testament accounts of the cross outline its bountiful provision. Stop and think about that for a moment. We all generically ascribe the verse *"by His stripes we are healed"* to our time around communion, but it is only one aspect of a plethora of more definitive promises awaiting discovery, beyond our potentially rote handling of this sacrament. Jesus encourages us to continually partake of the table so that we would access more of its provision.

Application

Have you experienced your heart burning within you as you discovered Christ in the Old Testament?

Why do you think Jesus linked the disciples' burning hearts with the taking of communion?

Could it be that we are settling for less than God planned by making communion a ritual?

Chapter 10

CROSSING JORDAN

Joshua 3:1-17

Reinterpreting Scripture in Light of the Cross

While the cross may be considered the doorway to the kingdom in terms of chronological access, it is also the eternal key to kingdom provision hidden in plain sight. To put substance into God's promises and provision, we do not have to travel to the far corners of the globe, we simply have to reconsider what we may have previously overlooked by getting caught up in the narrative. That narrative may be the story of people's lives, what's portrayed through a variety of different media, or as here, in Scripture.

The Kingdom Is Hidden in the Word

The Scriptures are deliberately sown with a plethora of treasures that are hidden beyond the grasp of carnal humankind. Just as Jesus veiled His instruction on the kingdom by using parables (Matthew 13:34), God has secreted the storehouses of heaven within the pages of His Word. This is why after teaching on the kingdom by only using parables, Jesus went on to describe the writer mentioned in the kingdom as one bringing out new and old:

> ...*Therefore every scribe which is instructed unto the kingdom of heaven is like unto a man that is a householder, which brings forth out of his treasure things new and old* (Matthew 13:52).

Jesus here described someone who is well-versed in Scripture being able to unlock layers of revelation, beyond a surface reading, and thereby bring forth the new from the old. In practical terms, this means well-known Old Testament passages, when revisited in light of the cross, open up new vistas of what took place that day. These hidden multidimensional truths were simultaneously part of the atonement but remain mostly unrecognized until now.

Due to the eternal nature of the kingdom, it is now possible to both plumb and activate the depths of the spiritual victory achieved in the cross. Things that were incomprehensible to those at the time who observed the event. Each Old Testament passage continually adds detail to reveal that God has set before us an incredible table of provision from which we are able to truly taste and see His goodness. Remember, all this is possible because the cross is the ultimate fulfillment of every previous victory, blessing, and miracle portrayed in Scripture.

Crossing Jordan

One such passage is found in the Book of Joshua, chapter 3. This is where the children of Israel crossed the Jordan River under Joshua's leadership. The Bible records that when the feet of the priests bearing the ark touched the river, the water did not merely part, rather it banked up all the way to a specific city.

Before we discuss what is revealed in its name, it would do us well, to consider what was in the Ark of the Covenant. The Ark contained a sample of the manna, Aaron's rod that budded, and the two tablets containing the Ten Commandments. From John's Gospel, we recognize that Jesus is the true Bread from heaven (manna); similarly, He is the Resurrection and the Life (Aaron's rod), and He is the embodiment and fulfillment of the Law (the Word). See John 6:51; 11:25; 1:11,14.

It is also important at this point to recognize that the name Jordan means death or descender. Therefore, the priests bearing the Ark, stepping into Jordan, portray Christ entering death. That in itself is a prominent signpost for us to stop here and dig deeper. On excavation, this particular record of events unearths a number of nuggets of kingdom treasure for its guests.

As the crossing depicts Christ entering death, the comment that they had *"not passed this way before"* (Joshua 3:4), suggests that just as the people of Israel were entering uncharted waters—in moving into the eternal kingdom, we are similarly traversing new ground. Therefore, the kingdom is not to be viewed, judged, or governed by our previous earthly experience. New concepts, such as our access by faith to the provision found in eternal time, are not necessarily wrong just because they are currently beyond our grid.

The preface to Israel's crossing says that the event would be marked by *"wonders among them"* (Joshua 3:5). For us, this means that entry to the kingdom brings us into the realm of the extraordinary. The miracle performed at the crossing was also to signal that God was among them and would without fail drive out its inhabitants (Joshua 3:10).

Why then, are we so surprised by resistance when it was always part of this forewarning? These words also hold a two-fold promise for us. Though there will be opposition, we are assured victory through His infilled presence. Knowing that the name Jordan means death, and that *"the wages of sin is death"* (Romans 6:23), when we come to read that *"Jordan overflows its banks in harvest"* (Joshua 3:15), we recognize that it is normal, that soul-winning and fruitfulness are accompanied with opposition and a flood of sinful activity.

Last, but certainly not least, Joshua 3:1-17 records that the waters of the Jordan did not merely part, they rolled all the way back to a town named Adam! When Jesus stepped into eternity, He not only made a way for us to enter, He also rolled back sin and its consequences—all the way back to the progenitor of humankind, Adam. That means that any generational curse that has been passed down through your heritage has no legal standing.

Application

Imagine you are in that parade of Israelites crossing the Jordan. You are promised wonders and His presence to accompany you. What does that look like for you?

What generational curse in your family has to be served notice, following the Jordan rolling back to the town named Adam?

Chapter 11

THE PRESENCE

We have seen that crossing the Jordan brought with it the promise of God's presence. There is a universal presence and a tangible, or manifest, presence of God. Adam and Eve hid and Jonah ran from the manifest presence of God. On the other hand, Jeremiah was speaking about the universal presence, or omnipresence of God, when he penned:

> *Can any hide himself in secret places that I should not see them? Says the Lord. Do not I fill heaven and earth? Says the Lord* (Jeremiah 23:24).

His tangible presence is a companionship and habitation all too readily forgotten and overlooked because of His invisible nature. It is, however, no less real than the material world around us, and something to be valued, sought, and nurtured.

Without Your Presence, I Don't Want to Go

Moses, as Israel's leader and a friend of God (Exodus 33:11) knew and so cherished, his Friend's presence that he refused to go up into the Promised Land without it:

> *And He said, "My Presence will go with you, and I will give you rest." Then he said to Him, "If Your Presence does*

not go with us, do not bring us up from here. For how then will it be known that Your people and I have found grace in Your sight, except You go with us? So we shall be separate, Your people and I, from all the people who are upon the face of the earth" (Exodus 33:14-16).

God's Presence Sets You Apart

These verses also explain that God's presence wasn't merely that of a traveling companion, it was what set Israel apart from the rest of humanity. As it did for Israel, God's presence still marks the grace of God, something not to be taken lightly. The example of Moses is mirrored in the confession of Samson to Delilah when he said:

...if I be shaven, then my strength will go from me, and I shall become weak, and be like any other man (Judges 16:17).

Samson's strength was due to the anointing upon him, which became evident when he failed to realize the Spirit had left him (Judges 16:20). God's presence did more than provide strength to Samson and make a way for Israel, He was Samson's Strength and his Way. Moses, in requesting His presence, set forth a foundational truth for those wanting to enter the kingdom. In fact, as radical a thought as it may be, His presence is not only needed to enter the kingdom, it is *the* kingdom itself. How is that so?

Kingdom Foundations

In the Book of Matthew, Jesus lays out the key foundations of the kingdom. He then expands on these buttresses before demonstrating them through His ministry. This substructure to kingdom living is laid out in the verses commonly known as The Beatitudes. These are then filled out in the instruction known as The Sermon on the Mount. Unfortunately, the common names given to these maxims is prone to cause us to stereotype their content and fail to plumb their true worth. The first and last of these precepts to kingdom living ends with the words "...*for theirs is the kingdom of heaven.*"

> *Blessed are the poor in spirit, for theirs is the kingdom of heaven. ...Blessed are those that are persecuted, for theirs is the kingdom of heaven* (Matthew 5:3,10).

These identical two phrases, bookend the material and tell us the scope and focus of the content. In Hebrew thought, these two markers are meant to grab our attention, and bring us in for a closer look. Without opening the whole passage, so we stay on the subject, take note that each of the eight precepts begins with the word *"Blessed"* in Matthew 5:3-10:

- Blessed are the poor in spirit: for theirs is the kingdom of heaven.

- Blessed are they that mourn: for they shall be comforted.

- Blessed are the meek: for they shall inherit the earth.

- Blessed are they which do hunger and thirst after righteousness: for they shall be filled.

- Blessed are the merciful: for they shall obtain mercy.

- Blessed are the pure in heart: for they shall see God.

- Blessed are the peacemakers: for they shall be called the sons of God.

- Blessed are they that are persecuted for righteousness' sake: for theirs is the kingdom of heaven.

The word "blessed" is the Greek word *makarios*. However, this word is based on the Hebrew word *asher*, which likewise means blessed or happy. This word starts Psalm 1, *"Blessed is the one...."* The word *asher* in Hebrew is made up of three letters: *aleph, sheen, reysh* (אֲשֶׁר). The first two letters spell out strong devourer, which is elsewhere interpreted as fire; and the last letter, *reysh,* means person or head. Therefore, the word *asher* means fire on the head, and in this context signifies the presence of God. That understanding is exactly what we see with the outpouring of the Holy Spirit on the Day of Pentecost. The fire on the head marked the union of God and humankind.

If we now bring that understanding back into the passage in Matthew, looking at the eight precepts that undergird the kingdom, we find all eight lead in with a blessing, the basis of which is God's tangible presence Himself. We could legitimately say:

The presence of God is with the poor in spirit, for theirs is the kingdom of heaven.

The presence of God is with those that mourn...

The presence of God is with the meek...

The presence of God is with those who hunger and thirst after righteousness...

The presence of God is with the merciful...

The presence of God is with the pure of heart...

The presence of God is with those that are persecuted for righteousness' sake,

for theirs is the kingdom of heaven (Matthew 5:3-10).

Therefore, there is a direct correlation between the kingdom of heaven and His tangible presence. Looking at these virtues, it is not so very surprising that Jesus said to Pilate, *"My kingdom was not of this world."*

A Glimpse at the Kingdom's Glory

This concept of His tangible presence being one with His kingdom can be challenging to our linear and finite thinking. For that reason, also consider that every kingdom has a level of glory associated with it. However, the kingdom of the King of Glory (Psalm 24:7-10), that's a glory beyond all glories and surpasses them all (Daniel 7:13-14). Jesus gave His disciples a glimpse of that kingdom when He performed the miracle of turning the water to wine; and thus, it is recorded that He *"manifested forth His glory"* (John 2:11). As was the case in that story, His glory is hidden until it is manifest through a representation of the cross. How does the wedding at Cana relate to the cross? Well, Jesus used an Aramaic idiom, at that time, when He said to His mother:

> *Woman, what have I to do with you? My hour has not yet come* (John 2:4).

Jesus wasn't primarily talking to Mary. He was speaking idiomatically to Jerusalem, because Jerusalem was known as the mother of Israel (Galatians 4:26). Jesus was in effect saying, *I have a rendezvous with Jerusalem, but not yet.* That awaiting, appointed meeting was at the cross.

Application

The presence of God sets us apart from the world. Take time to invite His presence right now.

Today, in a quiet moment, pull your thoughts back from the world around you and sense His presence.

Read through the Beatitudes and identify the virtues that are associated with His presence.

Chapter 12

THE FEARLESS GIRL

My heart has been stirred recently by church leadership, on repeated occasions, apologetically announcing to their congregations that they do not believe in a "prosperity gospel." Such comments perform a great injustice by indirectly reinforcing only the redemptive side of the cross, and negating the kingdom into which Christ has led us. Had their comments been part of the preamble leading to an offering talk, I could perhaps have understood their attempts to soften a request to "sow." Rather amazingly, their remarks appeared to come unsolicited and unaccompanied with such a connection.

Excess or Abuse?

I believe underlying this apologetic rationale are two lines of thinking, the first being an amends for blatant abuse. This is where prosperity is associated with and touted by those who manipulate their audience to justify their extreme pull for finances. It is important to make a distinction here between excess and abuse. Excess is not necessarily abuse. Our Father is a God of overflow (Psalm 23:5) who is able to do exceedingly abundantly above what we ask or think (Ephesians 3:20) and gives life abundantly (John 10:10). Abraham and Solomon were recipients of God's provision and as such were extremely wealthy. However, having excess may become abuse when there is no onward flow toward the work of the kingdom. In short, abuse is manipulation for selfish gain, with little or no outflow into other ministries working in the kingdom.

The Spirit of the World

The other influence that may lay behind an apologetic approach to giving is the spirit of the world that creeps and meanders its way in from ungodly associations warily proclaiming, "All the church is after is your money." While we know this is not true, the nagging cries may linger and give us reason to avoid openly asking God's people to invest in the work. The enemy who is behind the spirit of this world looks to put a stranglehold on the work of the kingdom by restricting financial flow.

Some pastors find themselves so on the back foot, a defensive stance, that they do not openly take up offerings but rather passively leave a receptacle at the rear of the building where people may leave a donation after the service. Perhaps such a stance could be justified by a repeated history of abuse; but for the most part, those who maintain this practice do so to not offend their congregations.

However, the Bible is an offense to the world and repeatedly displays the taking up of finances and provisions for the work of the ministry (Exodus 35:21-29; 1 Kings 17:11-12; John 6:9). Putting extreme cases of abuse aside for a moment, the giving of tithes and offerings is not about the church "taking" anything from its people, it's recognizing and acknowledging that it is God who gave the opportunity to gain provisions in the first place. Most of us earn money for the time we spend doing a job. So, the giving of it is an act of worship-filled service, spiritually declaring that what we do for a living is done unto the Lord (Colossians 3:22-23).

The Bronze Statue

Moving right along and bringing this into the interface between the two realms of heaven and earth is a bronze sculpture of a young girl—the Fearless Girl. Erected on the March 7, 2017, in the financial district of New York City, her positioning is such that she defiantly faces the Charging Bull of Wall Street. At 50 inches tall and weighing 250 pounds, she is diminutive compared to the bull, which symbolizes a rising and prosperous economic and financial sector. The sculpture was commissioned as a statement that women are a vital part of business leadership.

However, little did those who instigated her construction know that prophetically she is a declaration to The Mountain of Finance, the Seven Mountain Mandate, that the time has come to loosen the grip the secular world has had on the world's economy. In the Spirit, she represents an emerging and maturing prophetic church—the Bride of Christ—that is now being positioned to challenge the hold on finance held by secular society.

A Good Father Leaves an Inheritance

Coinciding with the fearless girl, the Bible says:

> *A good man leaves an inheritance to his children's children:*
> *And the wealth of the wicked, is laid up for the righteous*
> (Proverbs 13:22).

Here's the interesting thing, the word "man" is in italics (in the published text), which means it has been added to aid our understanding, it is not in the original script. This Scripture might well make sense with the word "man" injected until Jesus happens to say, *"There is none good but one, that is God"* (Matthew 19:17). So at its core, the verse really relates that *a good God leaves an inheritance to His children's children.* At this point, it is worth noting that the word "children" used twice here is the Hebrew word *ben,* which means son. So the verse legitimately may be translated to read, *A good Father leaves an inheritance to His Son's sons.* And who might that be? You and I!

Proverbs 13:22 continues by saying, *"And the wealth of the wicked, is laid up for the righteous."* Here we need to recognize that the word "wicked" describes those who miss the mark; and in the Book of Judges it describes slingmen who do not hit their target (Judges 20:16). The sling's motion scribes a circle—having no beginning and no end—and as such is a depiction of revelation from the eternal realm breaking through into this world and being relayed by the human spirit. The projectile that is cast from a sling is revelation being released as a word from God to combat forces that oppose His kingdom being established. It is this *rhema* or revelatory word that takes out the enemy.

The Fearless Girl sculpture on Wall Street is a prophetic enactment telling us that it is time for the prophetic church to start claiming her inheritance. Aligning with this is our verse from the Book of Proverbs, which now effectively says: *A good Father leaves an inheritance to His Son's sons, and the wealth of those without revelation is laid up for those with revelation.*

Application

Is there a financial strongman resisting you? It may be a mortgage, a job, a contract, a lease, a financial commitment, or the like.

Proverbs 13:22 is a word of revelation to be used against your spiritual foe.

Imagine this word is a stone in your sling. Get your target in mind (this is not a person, but a spirit behind the person, institution, or contract, etc.).

Arm your sling by turning it overhead.

Now, release the word of revelation by making a decree as you release the stone into the spirit realm, at the strongman resisting you. Make sure you watch the stone strike its target.

Now, thank God for His victory at the cross that made this possible.

Chapter 13

ONE MAN

Key to a discussion on the kingdom, and following on from the importance of revelation to enter, is the subject of *unity*. While your thoughts are likely gravitating toward this material addressing a corporate need, what I want to share here is, first and foremost, the gaining of vertical alignment at an individual level.

Gideon

The story of Gideon in the Old Testament provides the kick-off point for this expedition. Stuck in Israel's past glories and unable to apply faith for the nation's current dilemmas; God's dealings with Gideon, the yet to be, *"mighty man of valor"* furnish key insights for us. In the opening encounter with the Angel of the Lord, Gideon is told he will defeat the Midianites as *"one man"* (Judges 6:16). While ultimately this speaks of Christ within, the narrative beautifully presents metaphorically what this unity looked like for Gideon and his men.

Without doing too detailed an exposition, God first commanded Gideon to remove from his army those who were in fear of the awaited battle with their Midianite foe. Here, twenty-two thousand men left their ranks to go home. Why did God do this? Simply put, fear divides us. Though our mouths and actions may say otherwise, if fear is present in our hearts, we do not have the necessary foundation within to stand against the enemy.

In other words, if our inner self does not align with the outer, the outer self will fold when tested. God thinned Gideon's army further by the way each man chose to drink from a water source. So Gideon led the ten thousand men who remained to a stream where three hundred of them drank by bringing their hand to mouth and lapped like a dog. It was with these that God announced Gideon was to face his foe. Why was their method of drinking chosen as the arbitrator? Cupping one's hand to drink signifies collecting life-giving revelation from the Holy Spirit (the running stream) in the heart (the cupped hand), and raising it to be lapped with the tongue speaks of declaring (mouth/tongue) what is revealed.

In case we missed it, the Holy Spirit repeats the necessary elements again when the three hundred men face the Midianites. Here the three hundred are to copy Gideon in carrying a lamp concealed in a pitcher (an earthen vessel) in their left hand and a shofar (a ram's horn trumpet) in their right hand. On Gideon's signal, all are to break their pitchers and reveal the glory within, while blowing the trumpet at the same time. The lamp in the left hand is representative of the fire of revelation in the heart, while the trumpet in the right hand signifies faith in the Word of God in one's mouth.

Hopefully, you can see the lamp and the trumpet are a parallel of the earlier lesson where the living water placed in the heart is revealed in bringing it to their mouths. Thus, three hundred men defeated their enemy, as one man, as they each broke their pitcher (a depiction of casting off earthly constraints), and aligned their mouths with the glory revealed within. Similarly, each battle we face is turned in our favor and reveals God's glorious kingdom as we align ourselves progressively with each seed of revelation sown in our hearts.

Authority

A masterful demonstration of the need for inner agreement is found when Jesus was asked by the chief priests and elders by what authority He was moving in power (Matthew 21:23-27). On that occasion, Jesus responded to their question, by saying:

> ...*I also will ask you one thing, which if you tell me, I will likewise tell you by what authority I do these things. The baptism of John, where was it from? from heaven, or of men? And they reasoned with themselves, saying, If we shall say, From heaven; he will say unto us, Why did you not then believe him? But if we shall say, Of men; we fear the people; for all hold John as a prophet. And they answered Jesus, and said, We cannot tell. And he said unto them, Neither will I tell you by what authority I do these things* (Matthew 21:24-27).

Little did they know that they answered their own question. How so, you ask? In not being able to make a decision between the two, they spotlighted the enemy of authority, namely, double-mindedness. Jesus effectively answered their question without answering. What is communicated here but not said is that Jesus' authority came from receiving revelation in His heart, and then moving, acting, or speaking in alignment with it. The underlying problem for this delegation of elders was their greater concern for what others thought, rather than seeking the mind of God.

Pure in Heart

Undergirding this principle of aligning ourselves with revelation from heaven is one of the bedrock precepts known as The Beatitudes. It is here as one of the eight pillars of the kingdom that *"Blessed are the pure in heart..."* (Matthew 5:8) addresses the foundational need to be focused, resolute, and undivided in heart to see God's kingdom manifest. Jesus opens the meaning of this particular beatitude as He continues into the Sermon on the Mount. If the number of verses He dedicates to this particular theme is a measure of its importance, then we need to sit up and take note.

Starting in Matthew chapter 6, Jesus repeatedly shows how easily division robs us of a return as we go about kingdom activity. He addresses those seeking outward approval: as they give (Matthew 6:1-4); as they pray (Matthew 6:5-6); and as they fast (Matthew 6:16-18). Then more directly He spotlights issues of the heart in saying:

> *Lay not up for yourselves treasures upon earth...But lay up*
> *for yourselves treasures in heaven...For where your treasure*
> *is, there will your heart be also* (Matthew 6:19-21).

In context, Jesus continues by metaphorically describing the heart as the eye and emphasizes the importance of all that flows from it, by saying,

> *The light of the body is the eye: if therefore your eye is single,*
> *your whole body shall be full of light* (Matthew 6:22).

As this verse points out, singleness of vision within is critical to allowing the light of His glory to flood and flow from our being. If we are looking for the kingdom to manifest in and around our lives, the call is to avoid distractions that set up joint authorities in our lives. In a day and age where there are a plethora of things being presented to diffuse our focus and rob us of experiencing His fullness, those seeking the kingdom to manifest in their lives will heed Jesus' warning and recognize that *"No one can serve two masters..."* (Matthew 6:24). A divided heart is an ineffective and defeated heart.

In conclusion, Gideon did not set out to heal himself of self-doubt and fear. He became a mighty man of valor simply by settling in his heart that he had indeed heard from God and then aligned himself wholeheartedly with what he had heard. In doing so, God permitted him to share in the glory, in declaring, *"the sword of the Lord and of Gideon!"* (Judges 7:20).

Application

What would you say is the first requirement of getting vertical alignment within an individual?

What is it that disempowers people from operating in their God-given authority?

Thank God for the revelation He has hidden in Scripture to lead and guide us into the kingdom.

Chapter 14

DAVID AND GOLIATH

1 Samuel 17:1-53

Perhaps the greatest depiction of a victory of good over evil is seen in the classic battle of David and Goliath. Could this much-frequented scene hold secrets for us that we may have overlooked as witnesses of the cross?

Identifying the Cross

Our first charge would be to identify and prove this age-old story is indeed an interdimensional view of the cross. So to that end, let's see if there are elements here that echo that day.

Fortunately, as we scope the landscape there are signposts everywhere. First of note is the name David, which means beloved. Next, it should be noted that David, like Christ, was sent by his father to the battle. In his hand were loaves of bread sent from Bethlehem, House of Bread, in sync with Jesus who brought the true Bread from heaven. As an untrained and underaged lad fighting the Philistine champion, David could also be considered as a lamb to the slaughter, a lamb versus a roaring lion.

A little understanding of Hebrew tells us that the Philistines, being camped at *Ephes Dammim* (1 Samuel 17:1), literally the "Boundary of Blood," relates that they represent spirit forces arrayed against our advancement. The reference to blood must also surely speak of that day awaiting when Christ's blood was to be shed for our redemption. The opposition David received from his eldest brother, Eliab, paralleled the resistance Jesus received from the spiritual leadership of the household of God.

Facing Goliath

It is this level of parallel that beckons us closer to take a deeper look. Goliath's challenge and attire are incredibly informative. Knowing that Israel's sacrificial altars were made of brass means that Goliath's armor—being clothed from head to foot in brass—symbolizes he had set himself to judge Israel. His call to face *a man* among Israel not only hints of satan's rendezvous with the Son of Man, Jesus, it also tells us that the devil likes to face us in our weakest state, namely, our humanity. I hope you are beginning to see Goliath is a preview of satan. For us, his challenge to Israel is a forecasting move that forewarns us not to face him in our own strength.

The Spirit of Fear

Before we go too much further, we should note that before Goliath had uttered a word, he had a shield-bearer who went ahead of him (1 Samuel 17:7). Though a silent participant, make no mistake, he symbolizes a critical spiritual element of satan's modus operandi. He represents a spirit of fear that goes ahead of any battle to divide our head and heart. This is why when David arrived, Israel's soldiers were paralyzed, unable to go forward. It is also why the Scriptures record that the men of Israel were in *"the valley of Elah, fighting with the Philistines"* and yet remarkably there were no physical clashes taking place.

This is a good time for us to recognize and acknowledge that the battleground is the mind and that we need spiritual weapons to fight a demonic foe. Significantly, it was David's testimony that he had faced a lion and a bear that evidently convinced King Saul to give his consent to send forth the youngster. Yet, there is something deeper for us in his confession (1 Samuel 17:34-37).

In Scripture, it is the lion's roar and the bear's paw that are to be avoided (Revelation 13:2). The lion's roar symbolizes words of authority (Proverbs 28:1). To fully appreciate the meaning of the bear's paw, we need to consider that in Hebrew the word for "honey" is *devash* (דְּבַשׁ). The clue here is in the word's makeup, *devash* literally means "what the bear eats." Therefore, honey is what the bear eats. Now as honey in Scripture symbolizes revelation (1 Samuel 14:27; Ephesians 1:18), the bear's paw is to be avoided because it steals revelation from our hearts. This means, while the lion's authority attacks the head, the bear's paw attacks the heart. David's conquest over both lion and bear means that he was unaffected by fear, and thus not divided, and able to stand against Israel's foe.

Clothed in Him

David recognized that this was not primarily a physical fight and that the battle is the Lord's. As such, he was not reliant on conventional weapons (1 Samuel 17:47) and refused the offer of Saul's armor (1 Samuel 17:39). Instead, he came against the Philistine *"in the name of the Lord"* (1 Samuel 17:45). We could easily miss that the word "Lord" in Hebrew is *Yahweh,* comprised of the words: *Yod, Hey, Vav, Hey.* This is extremely significant in confirming that the scene prefigures the cross. *Yahweh* in Hebrew literally spells out: Hand, Behold, Nail, Behold!

Although somewhat veiled, if we put this in our terms, he is nonetheless saying, "Behold the hand, Behold the nail!" It is now becoming clearer that this contest hides more than we may have previously appreciated, and that we are viewing the epic battle that took place at the cross. By coming in God's name, David is effectively clothed in Christ and demonstrating for us our need to be bearers of the tangible presence.

Why Five Stones?

You may have heard David selected five smooth stones because Goliath had four brothers. While there is merit in that argument, the context suggests another line of thought, providing a better reason. Do you remember that Goliath was clothed in brass and that in doing so he was looking to judge humankind? The five smooth stones are God's response. On the heart of God are the twelve tribes of Israel, as signified by the high priest's breastplate. The five stones symbolize the first five sons of Jacob. They are smooth because through hardship they were to become suitable instruments for the Master's use.

The first five sons are Eliab, Simeon, Levi, Judah, and Dan: their names mean Behold a son, Hearing, Joined, Praise, and Judge. What does that sequence of name meanings spell out? It says, Behold a son, hearing and joined in praise brings judgment. In response to the devil's desire to judge humankind, the stones signify God has countered with a judgment of His own. If we had harbored doubts as we ventured out to uncover the cross in this story, they have surely been dealt a silencing blow with every new wave of revelation.

Plundering Tents

Notice, if you will, that David does not merely face Goliath, but runs at the whole Philistine army (1 Samuel 17:48). His victory over Goliath caused a tsunami among their ranks. Likewise, Jesus' defeat of satan means the enemy's house of cards has fallen. However, Israel's soldiers were not passive after the giant's fall, they went forward and plundered their enemies' tents (1 Samuel 17:53). Similarly, we are to take back our inheritance in the promises of God, which demonic forces have camped upon.

Goliath's Sword

While you are probably picking up gems along the way and hungering for more, we need to bring this episode to a close. David downed Goliath with a stone from his sling. As previously explained, the sling as a concave vessel represents the heart and the stone is a *rhema* word from God coming from the eternal Spirit of God to bring judgment. Nevertheless, the stone did not kill Goliath. What was it that killed Goliath? David came to the body of Goliath and drew the giant's own sword and used that to cut off his head.

Goliath's sword is the Word of God satan uses to accuse and judge us. It is important that we recognize this. Jesus, in like fashion, as the only Man without sin, has fought the enemy using satan's own weapon, *"and triumphed over them in it"* (Colossians 2:15). This is the only ground on which we stand. In Christ, we are privileged, like David, to say the battle is the Lord's, and in enforcing this victory, "The Lord rebuke you, satan!"

The Fruits of Victory

Finally, in defeating Goliath, David was promised riches, the king's daughter, and his father's house to go tax-free. The king's daughter speaks of Christ's union with us, the church. As His bride, spiritually we have access to all His provision, including all kinds of wealth in land, possessions, cattle, and descendants. Our tax-free component means the enemy can no longer use the debt of guilt, shame, or condemnation through something we or our descendants may have done as an account to hold us as his slaves.

Application

Why was David's killing of a lion and a bear a prerequisite to his facing of Goliath?

Recognize, in judging Christ, the devil was judged and lost the court battle.

Never try and stand against an attack in your own strength. Call upon God to clothe you with His presence.

Praise God in the darkest hour and He will fight your battle.

Don't be passive in reclaiming what is rightly yours. Identify it, and clothed in Christ, take it back.

Using your imagination, picture you are partaking of the King's promises. What would that look like for you?

Chapter 15

WHY DID HE WAIT?

John 11:1–12:11

Things didn't go exactly as they had planned for Martha and Mary. They had sent for Jesus while Lazarus, their brother, was sick; but alas, their brother had been dead four days before He finally arrived. Didn't He say their brother wouldn't die? At least that was likely what they heard when the messenger returned with His promise, *"This sickness is not unto death, but unto the glory of God"* (John 11:4).

Defying Expectation

The story of Lazarus immediately presents us with a contradiction. Jesus waited two more days in stark contrast to human expectation before starting out to remedy the situation for a family He clearly loved. The incongruity is staggering. Why did He wait? Was He merely stalling to amplify His power beyond the grave? Or was He, as some would say, challenging rabbinic teaching that the human soul leaves the body after three days?

While one or both of these answers may satisfy an initial inquiry, neither truly reveal the hidden path the Holy Spirit wants John's readers to travel. Unlike his synoptic counterparts, the signs chosen for inclusion in John's Gospel are limited, deliberate, and linked to convey a much deeper line of truth. The other Gospel writers also record Jesus raising people from the dead (Mark 5:35-43). They even explain it to be for God's glory (Luke 7:16). So what sets this episode apart? Why is this event assigned by John as the seventh sign?

To answer these questions, we need to open our hearts to a greater hidden truth by looking at the passage afresh, with our spiritual eyes open. Up front, the narrative that unfolds in John chapter 11 does supply answers to these questions, and in particular, why did Jesus wait two more days. It does so by openly stating:

1. He loved Lazarus (John 11:5),

2. that the glory of God would be manifest (John 11:4), and that He waited (John 11:6),

3. so that His disciples would believe (John 11:15).

Yet, these responses potentially pose even greater questions than they answer. While raising someone who has spent four days in the grave is significant, the true depth of this passage is not plumbed without a broader appreciation of all that is raised above, together with a contextual understanding of the obscure poetic language Jesus uses on the way.

The Underlying Plot

Many believe that John announced that it was Lazarus' sister Mary who anointed Jesus and wiped His feet with her hair, because the story was well known before John wrote his account. While his mention of Mary does introduce a known character, more importantly, it also serves to bookend with its counterpart, the actual anointing in John's next chapter, the opening and closing boundaries of this incident. These bookends, which are a Hebraic poetic literary device, help the reader identify the true extent of the underlying subject of the passage. This means the lesson of John chapter 11 does not close until John 12:11.

Why is this important? If the passage were to be closed off at the end of chapter 11, the reader may readily miss the point that after his resurrection, Lazarus is sitting at the table with Jesus. They may also miss what is communicated in the value assigned the oil by Judas Iscariot. Effectively, the two mentions of "anointing" mark the beginning and end of Jesus' life; and thus, His life purpose and mission are somehow portrayed in the raising of Lazarus. For this reason, John deliberately includes Caiaphas' prophecy of the need for Jesus to die between these two markers:

> *And one of them, named Caiaphas, being the high priest that same year, said unto them, You know nothing at all, nor consider that it is expedient for us, that one man should die for the people, and that the whole nation perish not. And this he spoke not of himself: but being high priest that year, he prophesied that Jesus should die for that nation; and not for that nation only, but that he also should gather together in one the children of God that were scattered abroad* (John 11:49-52).

Though it is Caiaphas delivering the words to lead the plot against Christ, John records them as a prophecy, to reveal that it is actually God orchestrating His greater purposes through Jesus—who is both called and chosen (Matthew 20:16; 22:14). Therefore, running in sync and beneath the drama that engulfs Martha, Mary, and Lazarus is a hidden and deeper message outlining the redemption of humankind.

Once this is understood, Jesus' statements like, *"This sickness is not unto death, but unto the glory of God"* start to make sense. The word "sickness" can legitimately also be translated as weakness, and thus Jesus' statement that, *"This weakness is not unto death..."* begs the question, what weakness? What weakness in humanity leads to death? The answer, of course, is that sin leads to death (Romans 6:23). Therefore, before Jesus even starts out on the road to the Bethany, He is declaring a change is at hand. His life purpose was to deal with the sin issue and thereby redeem humankind.

The apostle John is also responsible for telegraphing that in the process Jesus would also cleanse the human temple in preparation for His Spirit. He does this by relating that Jesus cleansed the earthly temple, built by Herod, at the beginning of His ministry (John 2:13-22). Whereas the synoptic writers record that Jesus purged the temple at the close of His ministry (Matthew 21:12; Mark 11:15). Again, the two events are bookends relating that He not only will deal with sin but will also clean up the human temple in the process.

Continued in the next chapter...

Application

While the chapter and paragraph headings inserted by publishers in our Bibles help us readily locate certain incidents in Scripture, unfortunately, they also have the propensity to condition us in our reading. If you want to go deeper than the surface narrative, you should try to ignore the paragraph titles, as they will blindside you to a deeper truth. Also, read broader than the scholarly-placed chapter endings as they often limit the field of exploration.

Caiaphas prophesied of Jesus' death, and he didn't even know God was using him. Has God used unbelievers in and around your life to speak prophetically into your situation?

From Jesus' response to their brother's sickness, Martha and Mary most likely thought their brother wasn't going to die. How much does our own agenda influence what we hear God say?

Chapter 16

WHY DID HE WAIT? CONTINUED

John 11:1-12:11

...Continued from the previous chapter.

Cohabitation

Jesus' seemingly random reference to walking in daylight, unless one should stumble at night, also comes into focus, when we understand there is another script being outworked beneath the surface here. However, unlike His previous indirect reference to sin and death, here His words take us deeper. He does this by suggesting that inner vision is required and that as, *"the Light of the world,"* He will ultimately cohabit with humankind when He says:

> *Are there not twelve hours in the day? If any man walk in the day, he stumbles not, because he sees the light of this world. But if a man walk in the night, he stumbles, because there is no light in him* (John 11:9-10).

This plan of cohabitation is God's masterstroke, where His glory would be manifest through His children *"as the waters cover the sea"* of humanity (Isaiah 11:9; Habakkuk 2:14). This also provides closure on the last part of Jesus' declaration, *"This sickness is not unto death, but unto the glory of God."* Jesus would not only meet God's judgment for human's propensity to sin, but would also in the process provide the means for humankind to be recipients of the presence of God. That, which initially looked like an unfulfilled promise of their brother's well-being, was ultimately fulfilled at a scale totally unimaginable to Martha and Mary.

From Glory to Glory

This is why the Holy Spirit, through John, chose this incident as his seventh sign. John's seventh sign relates the resurrection of the human spirit, while his *"beginning of miracles"* at the turning of water to wine, marked humankind's infilling with the joy of the Holy Spirit. Notice, if you will, that the first and seventh signs are both marked by the manifestation of *glory*.

> *This beginning of miracles did Jesus in Cana of Galilee, and manifested forth his glory; and his disciples believed on him* (John 2:11).

> *When Jesus heard that, he said, This sickness is not unto death, but for the glory of God, that the Son of God might be glorified thereby* (John 11:4).

The two miracles envelop the signs between—in glory—and in doing so, signal that all seven signs are related and are now complete. The fact that both the first and seventh signs hide facets of the cross relates that the cross is the epicenter of His glory. For in it, the heart of God is revealed.

Three Hundred

What is the significance of Judas Iscariot's suggestion that the oil could have been sold for 300 denarii? Three hundred is the number associated with the glory of God. This comes from the days of Solomon who had 300 golden shields made for the house of the Forest of Lebanon (1 Kings 10:17). History relates they were placed on the outside of the tower, where they radiated the sun's rays throughout the land, signifying the glory of God in residence. Judas' objection to the use of the anointing oil, wanting it sold for 300 denarii, says poetically that greed will forfeit the glory for selfish gain (John 12:5-6).

Why Did He Wait?

Why did Jesus wait two more days? The apostle Peter tells us *"that one day with the Lord is as a thousand years, and a thousand years as one day"* (2 Peter 3:8). As Jesus waited two days after hearing the news of Lazarus' sickness, the Lord waited 2,000 years from Adam's Fall before setting into motion His plan of redemption through Abraham's lineage. Just as Lazarus had been dead for four days before Jesus arrived, He likewise waited 4,000 years before being born of Mary. Lazarus himself is thus a personification of the human spirit, which had been dead since Adam's fall in the garden. The fact that Jesus' reference to Lazarus' condition as *"sleep,"* now telegraphs the temporary nature of the Fall in the mind of God.

Martha and Mary

Martha, who projects the resurrection to some future time, is a personification of the human body, the physical being. She represents the material dimension of humankind, displaying a propensity for doing. Mary, on the other hand, is a depiction of the human soul, the inner self, thoughtful and devoted. Her tears and emotion are an expression of the inner life meeting its limit to understand, beyond reason, why such an event should happen.

Answering Unspoken Questions

John captures the hidden questions of the human heart when the Jews say, *"Could not this Man, who opened the eyes of the blind, stop this man from dying?"* (John 11:37). When we recognize that opening the eyes parallels the creation of light in Scripture, beneath the scene before us is the veiled question, "If God is the all-powerful Creator beginning with light, why didn't He prevent the Fall of humankind?" Following on from this is, "If God couldn't prevent Adam's Fall, then salvation is perceived to be God's plan B." The raising of Lazarus totally and unequivocally blasts any doubt about God's omniscience and omnipotence out of the water.

The resurrection of Lazarus declares that what looked like a mistake, an inability to meet the immediate need of man, was in fact, the greatest show on earth! God's love for humankind was greater than a temporary and superficial fix. This was His glory revealed for those with eyes to see.

Yes, Lazarus was allowed to sleep. Yes, God foresaw the Fall, and in it prepared a greater victory. You see, the four days are as the 4,000 years before Christ's birth. In that time the history of humanity's redemption is cultivated through the nation of Israel. Every law, prophecy, event, incident, and feast, when interpreted in the light of the cross, is not merely a type or foreshadowing of that event. Each is a spiritual dimension of the victory of the cross, that the Gospel writers could not see and document in His crucifixion. You see, the eternal kingdom bridges the barrier of chronological time, and in doing so provides access to God's goodness played out in every pre-cross event of Scripture. This is what puts substance into Paul's words:

For all the promises of God in him are yes, and in him
Amen, unto the glory of God by us (2 Corinthians 1:20).

Jesus waited so that you and I would inherit this glorious kingdom, having tangible provision to wrap our faith around. David's victory over Goliath preceded the raiding of the tents of the Philistines. The crossing of the Red Sea depicts a boundary of blood around the redeemed that the devil, Pharaoh, cannot cross. The bronze serpent on the pole relates that if we break through the hedge God has placed around us, there are yet further depths of renewal in turning to the cross. The offering of Isaac shows us that in His victory, He has given us authority—the gates of our enemies—over every stronghold.

And, of course, Isaiah 53 declares that every sickness and disease no longer has authority to reside in your body. The list could go on and on. That's why Lazarus is finally found seated with Jesus, because it announces that the table of His provision is now fully available. He waited because, in His love, He was providing an innumerable body of believers, with an incomprehensible banquet of provision beyond a mere delivering from the fires of hell. He waited so that you and I would be carriers of this glory to the whole of humankind, as the waters of revelation cover the sea of humanity.

Application

Reread the last two paragraphs.

Jesus is worthy of praise!

What other Scriptures go off inside you as you read these two discussions on Lazarus?

Are you drawn to look at the rest of John's signs to see what they hide?

Chapter 17

SAMSON

Hidden in the biblical record of the life of Samson, one of the least understood heroes of faith (Hebrews 11:32), is a rare insight into the events surrounding the cross and its aftermath. In particular, the episode where Samson kills a thousand Philistines is very rich in inter-dimensional truth (Judges 15:9-20).

The Mouth of Heaven

The record of events began with the Philistines, who went up and encamped in Lehi in the district of Judah. This positioning of the enemy is deeply significant in light of the events that followed. The importance of this placement is suggested by Samson's latter embellishment of the name (Judges 15:17). Lehi means jawbone and thus also carries the thought of mouth and words. Philistines entrenched in this location represent evil spirits blocking the portal or mouth of heaven.

The story continues when men from the tribe of Judah came and bound Samson using two new cords, and delivered him into the hands of the Philistines (Judges 15:13). This scene matched the action of

Jerusalem's leadership who employed two false witnesses to accuse Jesus of blasphemy (Matthew 26:60). This was before handing Him over to the Gentiles who were pawns moved by spiritual forces, set against humankind's access to heaven.

Jawbone Height

In bringing Samson up to Lehi, we see Jesus hanging between heaven and earth on a Roman cross. It is here, in breaking free of the cords that bound him, Samson paralleled false accusations laid upon a sinless Christ. Like the donkey, Jesus is our Burden Bearer and Suffering Servant. According to Isaiah, a thousand men is as a nation (Isaiah 60:22). So, Samson's slaying of a thousand Philistines with the jawbone of a donkey at Lehi (jawbone), is not only a display of God's poetic justice, it also echoes God's triumph over a nation of demons through the Servant Word (Colossians 2:15). Cementing the scene, as one of Christ upon the cross is Samson's cry, *"I thirst!"* (John 19:28).

God's response was to split open and pour water with force from the fallen jawbone. This happened at a place called Ramath Lehi, meaning words from on high, and En Hakkore, meaning the well of the caller, displaying the definitive opening of heaven through Jesus' sacrificial act. These descriptions also clarify the portal through which heaven now makes entry into our world, namely through the mouth of believers hearing from God. It should be noted that the Bible records the well is there *"till this day"* (Judges 15:19), meaning heaven is now forever open for business.

This incident is brought to a close with the words, *"And he judged Israel in the days of the Philistines twenty years"* (Judges 15:20). The normal reign of God's appointed leaders was forty years. While this closing statement could be interpreted as Samson falling short of what was intended, it may be otherwise. When considered in the light of Luke's opening statement in the Book of Acts, *"...of all that Jesus began both to do and teach"* (Acts 1:1), it may be that Samson's short leadership as judge points to Jesus now completing His ministry through us.

Visiting Hell

Following this scene, which reveals spiritual insights not seen by eyewitnesses at the cross, is a bizarre episode where Samson visited a harlot in Gaza. When we simply lay a verse or two from the Book of Proverbs over this passage, we unexpectedly discover it to be a continuation of what took place beyond the cross. Solomon wrote:

> *A woman with the attire of a harlot...is the way to hell, going down to the chambers of death* (Proverbs 7:10,27).

And further,

> *For a whore is a deep ditch; and a strange woman is a narrow pit* (Proverbs 23:27).

Thus, Samson's visit to Gaza, which means stronghold, is a picture of what took place beyond the grave—when Jesus entered into hell. Now our appreciation of the scene changes completely. It is here that the Holy Spirit records Samson was there *"all the night"* twice, before declaring at *"midnight"* that Samson arose. Though Samson was only there overnight, the passage is recorded in such a way to parallel Christ's three nights in hell. Samson broke out of Gaza with the doors, two doorposts, and the locking bar on his shoulders. He took them to the top of the hill at Hebron. In doing so he revealed the authority transferred in the eternal gospel.

Hebron means union or association, and speaks of Christ's enthronement at the right hand of the Father. The two doorposts are sin and death, while the locking bar is the law that would otherwise hold us (Romans 8:2). Truly, *"the gates of hell shall not prevail"* against the church founded on the Rock of the finished work of Christ (Matthew 16:18).

Life and Death in the Power of the Tongue

I love this passage we're examining from Judges 15 and 16, not the least because hidden beneath the narrative that would otherwise be viewed with disdain, is a treasure trove of spiritual bounty. The hurling of the jawbone, which burst forth water from Lehi, depicts Jesus' death and the consequent unlocking of the well of heaven. It is here that Samson's desperate plea for God to meet his thirst is not merely a foreshadowing of Christ's later cry, but is rather a display of the vehemence of the Godhead's desperate desire to open heaven's reservoir to humankind. This passage also reveals the door through which heaven, and for that matter hell, is ushered to earth through the portal of our mouths. Thus, as heirs, in leaving us an inheritance, it is imperative we align the water of our words with the revelation He releases to see it materialize.

Resurrection Authority

Finally, Samson's destruction of the gates of Gaza depicts the dismantling of hell's legal authority. Thus, sin, hell, and death no longer have the power to hold us, and this narrative is actually a powerful tool for us, God's children, to meditate upon to see the power of God manifest through resurrections from the dead.

Application

Please read Judges 15:9–16:3.

Samson carried Gaza's gates upon his shoulders. Considering Isaiah 9:6, what is conveyed in this action?

Use your imagination to picture Samson busting out of Gaza.

Chapter 18

DAVID'S MIGHTY MEN

2 Samuel 23:8-17; 1 Chronicles 11:10-19

When we discussed the battle between David and Goliath, we discovered that the Philistines were encamped at a place called Ephes Dammim. Ephes Dammim and Pasdammim both mean the Boundary of Blood, and as such represent the line between this realm and eternity. This is simply because, if enough blood is spilled, we pass through death and cross over.

Another scene where we encounter Philistines entrenched at Pasdammim is found in the record of David's Three Mighty Men in First Chronicles 11:10-13. This discovery, found close to David's thirstful cry for water, again suggests that the passage likely holds yet more interdimensional secrets hidden in the cross. Up front, however, let's recognize that these men existed and physically achieved what was recorded about them. Nonetheless, it's what the Bible encodes beneath the story that holds its true wealth. Though their exploits are recorded, first individually and then with what they achieved working together, it's what they did together that first draws us to recognize the narrative's potential.

Thirsting for the Well of Heaven

So, we are at the place where heaven meets earth; Christ in David, is thirsting for the waters of heaven. This is depicted in this narrative, as Bethlehem, where there is a well. David is figuratively a picture of Christ in a stronghold—though Adullam was David's safe haven. In this context, his cave is a picture of Christ under the earth while the Philistines are evil spirits entrenched around the entrance to heaven, "dug in" to stop humanity from drinking from its provision.

How is Bethlehem representative of heaven? Bethlehem means House of Bread, and hopefully you recall that Jesus declared that He was *"the living Bread"* from heaven (John 6:51). Therefore, the true Bethlehem is where He came from—heaven. The scene is filled out by recording that the Philistines, while having a fortified military post, a garrison, at Bethlehem, were camped at the valley of Rephaim, and it was harvest time. Rephaim means giant, and thus their encampment relates they are holding the upper hand in the hearts of men. The fact that it was harvest time reminds us of when Israel, under Joshua's leadership, crossed the Jordan River to enter the Promised Land.

What do we see in David's men bringing him water from the well by the gate? (2 Samuel 23:15-16.) We see two things taking place. First, we see Jesus symbolized as the water of God's Word become flesh and blood, being poured out for us as an offering (Psalm 22:14). And second, we see heaven opened and its life-giving waters, the waters of the Holy Spirit, poured out on the earth, representing humankind. The offering and the opening are coincident. Heaven is now open, and we seriously need to reconsider singing songs asking God to open heaven, because we are likely reinforcing a lie in our own hearts, if we give voice to such a denial of His power and grace.

Three Working as One

Why are three men involved in this very singular portrayal of Christ's death? The answer lies in their identities as portrayed through their previous exploits. It should be noted that the record of the mighty men's feats of bravery in First Chronicles marks the commencement of David's reign. Those in Second Samuel mark the close of his leadership over Israel. What does that communicate? Their bookending of David's reign suggests that they, or who, or what they represent, was in influence for the length of his kingdom.

It should also be understood that the record given in Chronicles is a more spiritual, esoteric, and moral one providing a divine perspective, compared with the account given in Samuel, which is more physical, historical, secular, and offers a more human perspective. This is relevant because in Chronicles we read that they *"strengthened themselves with him in his kingdom...to make him king"* (1 Chronicles 11:10). Therefore, given that Jesus is the ultimate fulfillment of what was promised in David, we begin to appreciate that what is communicated here, through the acts of these mighty men, must also have sway now in Christ's kingdom.

The First Man Sat in the Seat

Who are the three mighty men? Looking at a composite of their individual acts of bravery provided by the two books, we discover a number of insights to their representative true identities.

Here, it should be noted that after the acts of bravery of the second and third men, that it is recorded, *"the Lord brought about a great victory"* (2 Samuel 23:10,12). While for some reason that credit is not given to the first of the three men who sat in the seat as the chief or head of the three.

Of this particular character, it is stated he had killed 800 or 300 at one time according to the separate accounts (2 Samuel 23; 1 Chronicles 11).

Eleazar's Hand Stuck to the Sword

Let us hold off on identifying the first man for a moment, while we look a little closer at the other two men. It is rather pointed that Eleazar, the second of the three men, whose name means helper, was also with David, meaning beloved, when everyone else had fled the scene. It is written that he *"arose"* and *"struck"* the Philistines *"until his hand was weary, and his hand stuck to the sword."* That's an interesting choice of words in light of the apostle Paul's reference to *"the sword of the Spirit, which is the word of God"* (Ephesians 6:17). Could it be that Eleazar is in fact a picture of the Holy Spirit who was with and in Christ, while everyone else deserted Him at the cross?

Shammah Placed Himself in the Middle of the Field

What about Shammah, the third of David's mighty men? His name means fame. This guy took on a troop of Philistines, who had gathered where there was a piece of ground full of lentils. And again, it is recorded that the people had fled from the Philistines. Shammah put himself in the middle of the field and defended or delivered it as he killed Philistines. Who is it whose fame spread because of the miracles He was performing (Matthew 4:24; 9:26,31; 14:1)? Who positioned Himself in the midst of humanity and defended both the seed of men and the seed of God's Word? Who was it that the enemy surrounded, gaping at Him as bulls of Bashan (Psalm 22:7,12-13)? Who did everyone desert in His hour of need (Matthew 26:31-35)? And finally, who made an open show of the enemy at the cross, disarming principalities and powers, making a public spectacle of them in it (Colossians 2:15)? It was, of course, the Lord Jesus Christ!

The Father

The greatest of the three, the Father (John 10:29; 14:28), is the Master of time (Acts 2:17), and He is also in the seat (Hebrews 8:1; Revelation 3:21). As this passage reveals, it was He who, through this one act in history, has established a new tribe (800), for His glory (300). The Father wrought something at the cross *one time* that not only changed the course of history, it could be considered the very epicenter of time. This is captured in the word "one" or *echad,* used here, which, rather than being a reference just to a singular moment, speaks of a unity or a unifying of time. So, this is not merely a single moment—it is that—but it is also a compound or composite moment.

In other words, this is an eternal moment that has within it every other significant moment recorded in Scripture. It is both singular and plural. Singular where Jesus' words, *"It is finished!"* mean the battle has been won. The devil, once and for all, has been defeated because God has removed and dealt with the barriers through the blood of His Son so that He and humankind may once again be one. And it is plural because at that moment, in that ultimate sacrifice, lies access to all of God's promises.

Battle Scenes of the Cross

Therefore, in scenes way beyond anyone's comprehension, as they looked on from the foot of the cross, battles were being fought in the spirit realm. Each of the individual battles of the mighty men—including their unified breakthrough together to draw water—relate interdimensional insights of the victory at the cross.

Little did we realize as we have read the Gospels, that hidden to the naked eye, beyond the shell of that battered sacrifice hanging on a tree, the whole Godhead was working together—including the Father and the Holy Spirit—to break through all the enemies' legal opposition and open heaven for humankind once and forever (John 16:32; 19:30; Luke 23:46; Colossians 2:9). Oh, how He loves us! And what assurance that brings.

God Looks for Someone Who Will Make a Stand

On a completely different level, the story of David's mighty men is also a timely reminder that while the masses are in flux and falling away, God is still looking for someone to make a stand, so He may empower them to do supernatural feats of strength and courage to reveal His glory.

Last but not least, there is a part we all have the privilege to play and it's found in the words, *"and the people returned after him only to plunder"* (2 Samuel 23:10). While on one hand we are only beginning to plumb the depths of the victory of the cross, on the other, scenes like this one reveal that it is our time to plunder, spoil, and reclaim our inheritance.

Application

Reread this study so that its truth begins to permeate you.

Take a little time and use your sanctified imagination to picture the battle scenes.

What does it mean to you that heaven is now open?

Chapter 19

CREATION

Genesis 1:1-19

The Lamb Slain from the Foundation

The last book of the Bible reveals that Jesus is *"the Lamb slain from the foundation of the world"* (Revelation 13:8). In saying that, it assures us that Jesus' death was not God's Plan B. When you think about it, that in itself is really good news. But wait, there is so much more hidden in the fact that Jesus' death envelops the whole Bible—that we are only now really beginning to understand as we grasp hold of the eternal interdimensional nature of the kingdom.

That said, it would not be unreasonable, then, to expect the creation week—which most fundamental believers consider the bedrock of our world—to contain a blueprint of Jesus' death as foretold by this verse in Revelation. Here we will only look at the first four days for brevity's sake, although a fuller description is found in *God's Prophetic Symbolism in Everyday Life*. So to begin, let us briefly look at a basic outline of the first four days of creation when:

1. God speaks lights into existence and divides the light from darkness.

2. God separates the waters above from waters below.

3. God gathers the waters under the heavens and causes the dry earth to appear. Plant life comes forth from the earth.

4. God sets the sun into the heavens to have dominion over the day. He sets the moon and stars into the night sky, to likewise have rule over the night.

If we now consider each of these days, looking at them through spiritual lenses. This is what we see.

Day 1

On day one, God revealed light to the world, which was formless and in the state of primeval chaos, shrouded in uncertainty, disorder, confusion-darkness, and emptiness-void. Darkness was on the face of the deep. By introducing light, He also separated and distinguished it from darkness. Spiritually this speaks of the manifestation of Jesus to a lost and broken world, whose hearts, the deep waters within, were veiled in sin (Proverbs 20:5). Jesus is the Light of the world (John 8:12). Like the introduction of a beam of light into a darkened room, His presence similarly divided and polarized people.

Day 2

Day two speaks of Jesus' death. How do we come to that conclusion? On every other day after He had created, it is recorded that God saw that it was *"good."* However, on the second day, God did not say it was good because the separation of waters signifies the separation of Father, waters above, from Son, waters beneath. Death is the separation of waters. Thus, when Moses led Israel through the Red Sea, and when Elijah led Elisha through the Jordan River, each crossing symbolized passing through the eternal barrier. That the second day represents death is further reinforced as we come to day three.

Day 3

On the third day, God gathered the waters under heaven into one place, and then let dry land appear. Then He imbued the earth to bring forth grass, herb that yields seed, and fruit trees that bring forth fruit according to their kind, whose seed is in themselves. Unlike the second day when there was no declaration of goodness, on the third day God saw that it was good twice.

The first recognition of goodness is because the earth coming out of the waters represents the resurrection. How is that so? Well, in Scripture man is presented as an earthen vessel, Paul makes reference to this analogy when he says, *"But we have this treasure in earthen vessels"* (2 Corinthians 4:7). This parallels Gideon, who had his men hide a flaming torch in an earthen vessel (Judges 7:16,20), and is tied to our origin in Adam, who was drawn from the dust of the earth (Genesis 2:7). Just as we baptize by full immersion, which depicts death, burial, and resurrection, the earth coming out of the water represents Christ's resurrection.

In line with the spiritual analogy that humans are as trees (Psalm 1:3), God's second mention of goodness, on day three, is tied to the inherent ability He has placed in His new creation, spiritually represented as trees, to produce fruit according to the seed carried within. Those seeds consist of the words we use and the foundation of our thoughts from which they emanate.

Day 4

Day four sees the establishment of the heavenly luminaries to divide the day from night, the sun to rule the day and the moon and stars to have dominion over the night. Following the resurrection, on the third day, these events portray the ascension of Christ, who is now seated and enthroned in heaven. According to Malachi, only those with faith can see it:

> But unto you that fear my name shall the Sun of righteousness arise with healing in His wings... (Malachi 4:2).

Jesus the Son is also *"the Sun of righteousness."* His victory at the cross and following ascension marks the establishment of His kingdom, together with His enthronement over it. All authority has been given to Him (Matthew 28:18). The physical elevation of the Sun above the earth depicts Jesus Christ's dominion over heaven and earth, this includes every earthly sickness and their roots in the spirit realm (Acts 10:38). The ultimate fulfillment of Malachi's word is through the cross. This means that Jesus is healing more now than when He walked the earth. That is worth thinking about. Therefore, if we will position our hearts to be irradiated, in His glorious presence, He will bring us under His wing for healing.

The Moon and Stars

This is truly wonderful! However, the fourth day has yet more in store. The moon and stars were also put into position over the night sky. What does this mean? Let us consider that night is the absence of light, and hence speaks of a time when Jesus is physically removed from the earth (John 9:5; 11:9-10). Also bear in mind, that when Jacob interpreted his son Joseph's dream, where the sun, moon, and eleven stars bowed down to him (Genesis 37:9-10), he recognized the moon and stars to be his wife and sons paying homage to Joseph (Genesis 37:10). Therefore, the moon in the night sky is a picture of the bride of Christ, the church, radiating the Sun's glory to a darkened world. The stars are a picture of us as Abraham's offspring (Genesis 15:5; Romans 4:13-16; Galatians 3:29).

In line with this, it is recorded that we are seated in heavenly places, a place of authority (Ephesians 2:6; Colossians 3:1). All of the heavenly luminaries of day four are also said to be for *"signs and seasons"* (Genesis 1:14). In Hebrew, these two words speak of miracles and appointed times respectively. Both corporately as the Bride and individually as heirs of the kingdom, we have been brought forth for *"such a time as this"* (I know that is now an overused cliché, yet an important Scripture found in Esther 4:14), to spread the knowledge of the glory of God in the face of Jesus Christ through signs and wonders.

God has encoded His gospel plan for humankind in the creation week. The first three days set forth Jesus' death, burial, and resurrection, leaving the next four days to describe the kingdom over which He and His heirs are to rule and reign. We are only mid-week, at day four, before Jesus' ascension, enthronement, and our positioning to be seated with Him are depicted. That means day four is the beginning of a whole new era.

We are missing half the story if we pack up shop at the cross. God has so much more in the gospel that we have been blindsided to when we stop at the blood's power to redeem us. The cross is a doorway beyond the eternal barrier, and the rest of the creation week is a description of the physical and spiritual areas over which we are to exercise dominion.

Application

The creation week gives us plenty of material around which we are able to exercise our imagination. Being metaphorically pictured as trees in the spirit realm (Psalm 1:3, Jeremiah 17:8; Isaiah 61:3), day three of creation reveals that we grow and reproduce according to the word-seeds that come from our own mouths. Take the time to repent and cancel any negative and restrictive words you have put in place over your life. Now, begin to confess that your life is destined to be fruitful and open the facets of provision hidden in the cross, by imagining scenes in line with these or other narratives He has opened to you.

Jesus has come in the flesh and *in Him* we have passed through the eternal barrier of death to be seated in heavenly places. Take time and soak in His presence; He is the Sun, and you are stars reflecting His glory. If you need healing, make it a daily habit to get in the *Sun,* and as you do so, imagine the warmth of His glorious rays penetrating your being.

The depth of separation experienced between Father and Son is a measure of His love for you (John 15:13). You were bought at such a high price that nothing in this earthly world has the right to accuse, condemn, and hold you to ransom (1 Corinthians 6:20). Just as each of the stars holds a special place, different hue and intensity in the heavens, you are now free to move into that area in the heavens that you were created to fill.

20

TREES IN THE GARDEN

The Return to Innocence

The Bible makes reference to the innocence of children, by describing them as those who do not yet know how to discern between their right hand and their left, as a metaphor for good and evil (Isaiah 7:16; Jonah 4:11; Hebrews 5:13-14). It was this level of innocence that Jesus made reference to when He said,

> *Truly, I say unto you, Except you be converted, and become as little children, you shall not enter into the kingdom of heaven* (Matthew 18:3).

When Jesus released this word to His disciples, He was directing them back to a state of *being,* found in the first man and woman, Adam and Eve. It was only after the Fall that Adam and Eve knew that they were naked and hid themselves from the presence of God. Before the Fall, like infants, they had no guilt and did not understand that their nakedness was socially inappropriate (Genesis 3:11). It was only after they had eaten from the tree of the knowledge of good and evil, that the Scriptures record that *"the eyes of both of them were opened, and they knew they were naked"* (Genesis 3:7). The eyes that were opened were their eyes to what had only been peripheral before the Fall—eyes that see the carnal world.

Here, as is sometimes the case when reading the Bible, God wants our attention drawn to what is unspoken. For example, Jesus said, *"A prophet has no honor in his own country"* (John 4:44). What was unsaid here was that a prophet is welcome elsewhere, where people are not familiar with him or her. For Adam and Eve, what was not said in the loss of their innocence, was the opening of their carnal vision, and with it the closing of their spiritual vision. This is endorsed by them perceiving their nakedness and being cast out of the garden, with the placement of an angel, who resides in the spirit realm, with a flaming sword, which is the word of judgment, guarding the way to the Tree of Life.

In parallel to Adam and Eve, children are innocent until they come to the place of the knowledge of right and wrong. Indeed, children see into the spirit realm of angels until the world around them closes that door (Matthew 18:10). This is the same principle that the apostle Paul is making reference to when he says:

> For I was alive without the law once: but when the commandment came...I died (Romans 7:9).

The Introduction of Boundaries

Unfortunately, for children the introduction of right and wrong is the point from which judgments begin to be made and the limitlessness of their hearts is beset with boundaries. Therefore, Jesus' reference to becoming as little children is an invitation to take off the blinders that restrict vision only to the material world and those things seen by the naked, the natural eye. The call to the kingdom is a returning to innocence—freedom from guilt—and the exercising of the inner eyes through a sanctified imagination (Matthew 6:33). This was life before the Fall. After the Fall, in stark contrast to its original state, we see that God observed that the imagination of the human heart was now *"only evil continually"* (Genesis 6:5).

The Imagination

It was because of this foundational role of the imagination that King David, a man after God's own heart, emphasized its importance in his final instructions to his son, Solomon. Thus, before he laid out the provisions and practical requirements for building the temple (1 Chronicles 28:10-11), he called his son to know God and to serve Him, because He *"...searches all hearts, and understands all the imaginations of the thoughts..."* (1 Chronicles 28:9). We traditionally interpret words like these as a warning of judgment. Perhaps, rightly so. However, what would happen if we were to view this verse with an understanding of the goodness of God? In this light, David's words take on a totally different hue, and would suggest that God has the capacity to use our imagination for altruistic and positive means (1 Chronicles 29:18).

The Hebrew word for imagination, *yetzer,* appears poetically and synonymously with *bara,* meaning to create, and is used to describe the forming, fashioning, and structuring of God's creative work. Like what is shaped by the hand of the potter. Therefore, the imagination plays a vital role with faith to see the *"things that do not exist, as though they did"* (Romans 4:17), materialize. Thus, when God announced that He would *"create man in His own image"* (Genesis 1:26), and voiced the same in the midst of the creation week, He did so endowing humankind with a creative imagination with the same purpose and capacity.

On one level, God has now returned us to the garden through the work of the cross. Our innocence or righteousness has been redeemed, and we are free to come to its center and eat from Christ, the Tree of Life. There are now also a plethora of trees available from which to feast around us. These are the multidimensional trees on which the Prince of Calvary died. They are shaped by our imaginative grasp of the victories they depict placed throughout Scripture.

Why Did God Allow the Fall?

The Fall of humankind came as no surprise to God. Why then did He allow its orchestration? Before the Fall, God and man were in relationship as two individual spirit beings. The cross was God's masterstroke, for through it, He paved the way for a new level of integration in which God would live in man. Not only that, but God now has multiple children, those with His DNA, who unlike Adam, have a permanent point of entry through the cross. And, in His likeness, He has furnished His sons and daughters with the means to create, *bara,* using the elements from the trees He has purposely provided.

Application

In the light of this discussion, what is the relevance of Deuteronomy 1:39?

Very often, what is not said is more important than what is expressed. For example, David did not put on Saul's armor because he hadn't tested it. What armor had he tested?

Be mindful of this subtle means of communication as you read your Bible. God will often hide gems in the text using this method.

If you do not recognize that you are an imaginative person, may I ask you a question? What do you do when a loved one is late coming home? You start to think on what could have happened, right? So, you do exercise your imagination! God wants you to harness that facet of your being, by imagining the kingdom. Choose a narrative we have discussed so far, and practice seeing the scenes.

Chapter 21

THE LANGUAGE OF THE KINGDOM

You would not plan on settling in a different country without first having some appreciation of the people's values, culture, and language. This is particularly true if you knew beforehand that their world was nothing like your own. Entering the kingdom of heaven is no different. We have grown up in an environment which is, for the most part, hostile toward God. As a consequence, its values and cultural norms require a change of thinking from our own. Having said that, it is not always easy to see the values that have permeated our mindset until we are confronted with its counterpart from the kingdom.

What makes our journey into the kingdom of heaven more interesting is that it is not physically separated from our own world. It's coexistence with our own means that language is one of the key elements that differentiate the two. While using the same host language, God is able to take it to a higher frequency, by use of Hebraic poetry. That's not poetry, as most of us would recognize it. We are not talking about the predominant use of rhyme, as found in English poetry.

God encodes and hides kingdom truth within the language that surrounds us every day, by extensive use of metaphor, personification, idiom, word plays, and parallelism.[1] The bookending technique revealed in a couple of the previous discussions is also one of its components. It has been said that poetry is not simply the use of higher language, it is the employment of higher vision because of its extensive use of imagery.

Parables

Jesus' use of parables in the Gospels is a classic example of how He is able to veil the kingdom from unbelievers with higher language. The Bible goes so far as to say that Jesus did not teach without using a parable (Mark 4:34). Why was that? That was because He was teaching His disciples the ways of the kingdom by using its language, yet at the same time keeping its treasure hidden from those with hard hearts. The poetic language of the kingdom is one of parables, riddles, and enigmas. It is not surprising, then, that the outpouring of God's Spirit is also accompanied by an increase of dreams and visions. Why? This is because dreams and visions make extensive use of metaphoric imagery. Dreams and visions are personal parables relating kingdom truths that are central to the dreamer.

Misunderstanding What God Is Saying

On a regular basis, God's use of poetic language causes many believers to fail to recognize the relevance of what He is communicating to them. We often miss that mainstream news stories—those that catch the attention of the whole world—hold within them kingdom messages. Another key avenue regularly overlooked are dreams. Some ministers write off all dreams as not from God because of an awkward dream they have personally experienced. While others go to the other extreme by prematurely publishing and projecting their dreams onto the world stage, when the content is really about something closer to home.

In the Gospels

Similarly, I have heard believers discount Jesus' teaching in the Gospels because they are not sure how to process some of His directives. While, thankfully, they do not take Him literally in regard to plucking out the right eye or cutting off the right hand, there is an uncertainty created in failing to realize He is using a key metaphor for dramatic effect. Plucking out your right eye and cutting off your right hand are references to your inner eye, that which your heart is focused on, and that which your heart is bent on doing (Matthew 5:29-30).

Think about it. God is not going to send Jesus to establish an eternal kingdom, 400 years after Israel's return to the land, without a message and purpose beyond that age. Though at that time He was primarily speaking to the Jews, He was also teaching those with ears to hear from every subsequent generation the values and language of the kingdom. Its language is poetic.

One Book Full of Provision

We are no longer bound by the law. However, the Old Testament, Gospels, and New Testament make up one Book. Our God, who is the Author, is beyond chronological time—being the same yesterday, today, and forever—and the kingdom He established through Christ's death upon the cross is eternal. This means that regardless of the legalism in which Israel was entangled, God has hidden manna on every page. This is particularly true in both the Old Testament and the Gospels, because they are rich in narratives. If we come to understand the language of the kingdom and its eternal nature, then we will find in the history it portrays, provision for today.

A Solid Foundation Creates a Stronger Building

The outbreak of supernatural phenomena and miracles the Church is currently experiencing is in keeping with an awakening to the twofold nature of the cross—redemption and kingdom. Knowing the importance of a scriptural footing, it is not so very surprising to recognize that God is also releasing fresh revelation of His kingdom founded on the Word. Revelation has deliberately been concealed within its pages so that God's children have available to them the means to identify resources and provision under the guidance of the Holy Spirit. It is this Bible-based revelation around which faith may confidently be exercised to see greater outpourings of His glory.

Application

When hearing from God through allegory and metaphor, either in the Bible, dreams, visions, or natural prophetic incidents, take your time in announcing what God is saying.

Read over some stories from Scripture that you haven't visited for a while and ask God to open them afresh, in the light of the cross.

ENDNOTE

1. Beale, Adrian. *The Mystic Awakening,* Destiny Image, 2014.

Chapter 22

JOSEPH

Genesis 40:1–41:52

The life of Joseph, Jacob's son, is a powerful portrayal of Christ's death, resurrection, and ascension. For that reason, it is the subject of many sermons. While there are multiple similarities in their journey we could explore, what interests us—once we have identified and acknowledged the overlay in the narrative—is a repeated theme that unlocks kingdom fruitfulness. Therefore, in an effort to keep things tight, this discussion will follow one avenue of thought.

Joseph and Jesus

Jumping into the story without too many preliminaries, Joseph is betrayed by his brothers and sold into slavery in Egypt where he is incarcerated for an offense he did not commit (see Genesis chapters 37 and 39). Jesus, was similarly betrayed by Judas, bound and falsely accused by His own people, and handed over to the Romans.

In prison, Joseph interpreted the dreams of two of Pharaoh's servants, one a bread-maker (baker) who was broken and hung on a tree (the cross), and another a wine-bearer (butler) who was in a pit before being lifted to his former position (the resurrection). Straight away these elements and the actions associated with them are a clear parallel of Jesus' death and resurrection. It was not for another *"two full years"* after his accurate interpretation of the dreams before Joseph was released to appear before Pharaoh (Genesis 41:1).

The completion of the second year, naturally enough, conveys Joseph's entry into the third year. Now, being mindful that in the Hebrew calendar there is a week of days, a week of weeks, a week of months and a week of years, Joseph effectively came out of his dungeon on the third day. Confirming the parity is the fact that the word used for dungeon in Hebrew also means death (Genesis 41:14). Hence, Joseph aligns with Jesus' resurrection in being brought out of prison, and his elevation to be Pharaoh's prime minister clearly echoes Christ's ascension and enthronement alongside the Father.

The Repeated Theme

With the overlay between the two clearly established, it is worth noting that when Joseph was summoned to appear before Pharaoh, he shaved and changed his clothes (Genesis 41:14). Though an audience before the king would be a good reason to be cleaned up, shaving also speaks of cutting off the flesh, and changing one's clothes of a new beginning, a new day.

This twofold theme is repeated when Joseph is released, and placed in the position to run the country. Here, he marries and has two sons. The naming of his offspring permanently records and telegraphs his journey. The first to be born is Manasseh, who bears this name because *"God…has made me forget all my toil, and all my father's house"* (Genesis 41:51). His second-born child is named, Ephraim, because *"God has caused me to be fruitful in the land of my affliction"* (Genesis 41:52).

Dealing with Issues

Even though by all accounts Joseph's outward life looked exemplary, in reality, like you and I, he was dealing with issues. Scripture records that he had received a word—his dream of his brothers bowing to him—yet had to undergo purifying in readiness for his future position (Psalm 105:19). If he had been perfect already, he wouldn't have needed refining. At the core of his being, Joseph had a pride problem, the process of his humbling can be traced through the diminishing ego-centric way he related to others. When he spoke to his brothers, he announced, *"I have had a dream"* (Genesis 37:6), to the butler and baker, he said, *"Do not interpretations belong to God, tell them to me"* (Genesis 40:8), and finally, standing before Pharaoh he affirmed, *"It is not in me, God will give Pharaoh an answer of peace"* (Genesis 41:16).

The Journey Out of His Own Prison

Remember, Joseph had experienced incredible injustice having journeyed from being the one-time-favorite of his father, through increasingly repressive steps, until he found himself bound in fetters (Psalm 105:18). So, what was it that brought about his necessary inner transformation? The primary vehicle God used to prepare Joseph was the deep emotional scarring he had experienced through the hands of his brothers (Genesis 42:21; 45:3; 50:15-18). He acknowledged this to be the case when he said, *"You thought evil against me, but God meant it for good"* (Genesis 50:20).

Did God cause his brothers to abuse him? No! Yet, knowing they would, God did not interfere with their free will. Instead, God knew that being increasingly reined in by his circumstances and Joseph's gifting and openness to the voice of the Spirit would bring him to an "Aha!" moment. The light really switched on for Joseph after he was forgotten by Pharaoh's butler. Hemmed in by circumstances against him, and battling harassing thoughts of injustice and revenge, as suggested by the naming of his first son, the living drama that was played out by Pharaoh's servants became the catalyst for heart change. A point in time came when he was forced to reflect on the dream revelation he had interpreted for the two men. When he did so, he recognized that the man being fed by demonic thoughts—birds flying and stealing baked goods from his head—didn't make it out alive.

Whereas the one who was released, was selfless, took no credit for himself, but gave all the glory to the one he served—depicted in his pressing grapes into a cup and putting it into Pharaoh's hand. Seeing himself in the picture, Joseph made a decision. He put to death the desires of the flesh fed by the enemy and chose to glorify the God of his father. He decided to let go of the past that he might embrace his future. This was more than a feigned change of heart to twist God's arm for a breakthrough. It was the establishment of a relationship (Genesis 49:22), because years later when he had the opportunity, he still refused to exact revenge, but deferred such to God (Genesis 50:19).

Giving Glory to God Under Trial

Most people are prone to complain when things do not go as planned, or adversity besets them. In naming his second son Ephraim, which signified being fruitful in the land of affliction, Joseph had not only reframed his situation, he also demonstrated the power of a heart set on giving glory to God under trial. The same enemy that feeds negative thoughts of destruction has no recourse but to withdraw against a person who positively praises God when tested.

Ultimately, Joseph tapped into a higher narrative than the one he had been experiencing. When he sought God, he saw through his circumstances and entered another dimension that wasn't moved by the facade-like offers and threats of this world. There is a point in time when you recognize that all you have been through, so far, has brought you to the place and position for which you are called. That is the place of peace. In that place, Joseph was no longer striving to be recognized or released, he was living on another level and had become a servant and friend of God.

Application

Joseph's passing through death and resurrection in parallel with Christ is more than a type and shadow of a future event. His story provides a multidimensional view of the path through the cross to the fruitfulness available on the other side. By embracing a bigger picture, he became a vessel for the glory of God and died to his past affliction by letting go of thoughts of revenge.

Are you willing to be more than a spectator of the cross by letting your grievances die with Christ that you may enter into your destiny and experience fruitfulness? Thank God for His revelation through Joseph. Determine to cultivate a lifestyle of glorifying God under trial.

Chapter 23

ANGELS

Jesus and Angels

While not making it a focal point, Jesus accepted angels as part of normal kingdom life. He was strengthened by angels (Matthew 4:11; Luke 22:43), was more than conversant with their function and make-up (Matthew 22:30), witnessed their audience before the Father (Matthew 18:10), spoke of their role in harvesting (Matthew 13:41,49; 24:31), linked them with the revealing of His glory (Matthew 25:31) and disclosed they accompany Him, making up His heavenly entourage (Matthew 16:27). On a corporate scale, when He was standing before Pilate, He also revealed that angels make up His army, and implied, at times, they may be called upon to change world events (Matthew 26:53; 2 Samuel 5:23-24; 2 Kings 6:16-17; Daniel 10:12-13).

The Centurion's Understanding

His recognition of the centurion's great faith, not only reveals a hierarchy in angel ranks, but it also highlights the servant and healing roles they perform. When speaking to Christ, the centurion said:

> *Lord, I am not worthy that you should come under my roof:*
> *but speak the word only, and my servant shall be healed.*

For I am a man under authority, having soldiers under me: and I say to this man, Go, and he goes; and to another, Come, and he comes; and to my servant, Do this, and he does it. When Jesus heard it, he marveled, and said to them that followed, Truly I say unto you, I have not found so great faith, no, not in Israel (Matthew 8:8-10).

The centurion was commended for great faith. A faith, strangely enough, not found among those from whom Jesus expected it. He understood that beyond the seen realm, the servants of the kingdom were there to perform God's word. When you think about it, the centurion's faith was modeled on a structure he was familiar with, but whose counterpart existed in the spirit realm. His understanding provided a structure about which his thoughts and imagination could frame up the invisible kingdom. Thus, he had effectively created a place in which his faith could be exercised.

Angels Ascending and Descending

In an earlier conversation, Jesus said to Nathaniel that he would see heaven opened and angels ascending and descending upon the Son of Man (John 1:51). His death has forever removed humankind's prohibition from heaven. Heaven is now open; and while we associate the title *Son of Man* as a direct reference to Christ, we need to remember that it does so, identifying Him with humanity—fully God and fully man. So, though we find it used extensively in the Book of Ezekiel, elsewhere the term *son of man* is used to show the frailty of humanity (Numbers 23:19; Psalm 8:4; 146:3; Isaiah 51:12; 56:2; Jeremiah 51:43). This means that Jesus was speaking on two levels.

First, Nathaniel would see the evidence of angels ministering through Jesus, but now with heaven open, heaven is interacting with earth through Christ's sons and daughters.

Angels Come to Earth through Your Mouth

This latter dimension, is further endorsed by the writer of the Book of Hebrews, who says, *"Angels...are they not all ministering spirits, sent forth to minister for them who shall be heirs of salvation?"* (Hebrews 1:13-14).

Here the phrase, *"sent forth to minister for them who shall be heirs of salvation,"* which is usually interpreted to mean angels go and search out the lost, actually carries a broader application. When the verse is literally understood, it reads, *ministering spirits, sent forth to minister through them who shall be heirs of salvation.* Now, the verse takes on a different hue.

Yes, angels are dispatched on salvation assignments, but more importantly, they are assigned to work with the saints. If I were to be deliberately thought provoking for a moment, I would say, "Angels come to earth through your mouth"! By this I mean that when we line up our mouths with God's revelatory word, angels go to work. This is in line with David, who lived and saw beyond his day (Matthew 12:3-5), and was singing prophetically when he said:

> *The Lord has prepared his throne in the heavens, and his kingdom rules over all. Bless the Lord, you his angels, that excel in strength, that do his word, hearkening unto the voice of his word* (Psalm 103:19-20).

David revealed that God's strong angels wait to hear revelation and move into action as it is released. Remember, David partook of God's eternal kingdom. He was living outside his chronological timeframe. Therefore, he is revealing something of the operating of the kingdom to us. Angels carry revelation from the throne of God and go into action to fulfill it when we open our mouths and release it.

We Are Kings (Hebrew: Melech)

The centurion understood something of the workings of the kingdom and for it was commended by Jesus as a person of great faith. His grasp of the operation of angels in the unseen realm is in accord with the two-fold nature of the cross. The apostle John pulls all of this together for us when he says:

> ...Unto him that loved us, and washed us from our sins in his own blood, And has made us kings and priests unto God and his Father; to him be glory and dominion forever and ever. Amen (Revelation 1:5-6).

According to this verse, we have been redeemed and washed clean through Jesus' blood, and now sit in heavenly places as kings and priests. In Hebrew, the word for king is *melech,* which is derived from two words, *mala* and *lecha.* These two words mean "word" and "Go, come now!" respectively, and are best paraphrased as, "Do what he says." Therefore, in choosing to record Jesus' interaction with the centurion, the Holy Spirit was pointing beyond that day, to ours. After setting ourselves to hear from God, we can demonstrate great faith, by imagining the rank and role of God's servants assigned to work in conjunction with us. Then, as kings, release His word to see the servants of the kingdom kick into action.

Application

Settle in your heart that angels are a normal part of kingdom life.

Including angels in the framework of the kingdom in our hearts allows them to work on your behalf.

Wait on God for revelation for someone else's kingdom need. Speak it and see angels go to work.

Chapter 24

THE SCARLET THREAD

Joshua 2:1-21

Exploring the personal interaction that leads to the salvation of one of the inhabitants of Jericho becomes the launching pad to confirm our place in the Abrahamic blessing. In overview, Joshua commissioned two men to spy out Jericho, before Israel crossed over the Jordan to take the land. Their mission was to report what they found. Once inside the city, the two men were evidently led of the Spirit to the house of Rahab, a prostitute. She sheltered them on the rooftop, hiding them under stalks of flax from the king's men searching for the intruders. As her house was on the wall, once the threat of detection had passed, Rahab provided a means of escape for them down through a window.

In the process of hiding and assisting them to return to Joshua, Rahab recounted how she had heard the power of the Lord had dried up the Red Sea when they came out of Egypt. In hiding Joshua's men, she not only revealed her heart belief, but also brought forth confession by saying, *"for the Lord your God, he is God in heaven above, and in earth beneath"* (Joshua 2:10-11). The incident closes with the scarlet thread used by Joshua's men to alight the city and depart that was left hanging from her window as a sign marking her home.

The window through which she sent them on their way is symbolic of the heart—as the heart is considered the seeing instrument in the spirit realm. Many may already understand the scarlet thread represents the blood of Christ applied to her heart as the means of salvation. What some may not realize is that the two men usually labeled as spies are actually two witnesses. They represent the head and the heart; it was the agreement of their testimony, and the scarlet thread, that saved Rahab and her household. In this regard, the apostle Paul wrote:

> *That if you shall confess with your mouth the Lord Jesus, and shall believe in your heart that God has raised him from the dead, you shall be saved. For with the heart man believes unto righteousness; and with the mouth confession is made unto salvation* (Romans 10:9-10).

The Red Sea Crossing and the Resurrection

In the Old Testament, the most often used reference to the power of God is found in the parting of the Red Sea. Its counterpart in the New Testament is the resurrection. The reason both hold this place of prominence is because they symbolize passing through and overcoming death. Therefore, Rahab's actions and confession after hearing of Israel's departure from Egypt through the Red Sea correlates with Paul's directive to the Roman church. In effect, she believed in Israel's deliverance from Pharaoh's clutches and resurrection to a new life, and displayed her faith in what she did and said.

Entering the Abrahamic Bloodline

While the scarlet thread is understood to be representative of the blood of Christ, it does so to reveal an opportunity to enter the Abrahamic bloodline. This is best illustrated at the place where the scarlet thread is first mentioned in Scripture. Judah, the son of Jacob, had two sons born to him by Tamar. At their birth, it is recorded:

> *And it came to pass, when she travailed, that the one put out his hand: and the midwife took and bound upon his hand a scarlet thread, saying, This came out first. And it came to pass, as he drew back his hand, that, behold, his brother came out: and she said, How have you broken forth? this breach be upon you: therefore his name was called Pharez. And afterwards came out his brother, that had the scarlet thread upon his hand: and his name was called Zarah* (Genesis 38:28-30).

Here, Pharez, whose name means breach or a breaking through, is given his name because he broke through between his brother's initial emergence and actual birth. Like Pharez, Rahab, a Gentile, broke through to be implanted into the bloodline leading to Israel's Messiah. Her demonstration of faith bypassed both the biological and religious requirements to be an Israelite. She qualified to become a spiritual Israelite, just as the apostle Paul would later come to explain, *"they which are of faith, the same are the children of Abraham"* (Galatians 3:7).

A couple of generations later, Ruth, a Moabitess, is similarly engrafted into the same bloodline through a demonstration of faith. Linking the two episodes is a declaration given by witnesses at the gate of Jerusalem. These bless the union of Boaz and Ruth by saying, *"...let your house be like the house of Pharez, whom Tamar bore unto Judah, of the seed which the Lord shall give you of this young woman"* (Ruth 4:12).

In a similar fashion, Ruth also became a vessel for the promise given to Abraham. In confirmation, the New Testament records that both women, who were considered aliens of Israel, became vessels of God, and are honored in the seed-line of Christ:

> *And Salmon begat Boaz of Rahab; and Boaz begat Obed of Ruth; and Obed begat Jesse; and Jesse begat David the king...* (Matthew 1:5-6).

Rahab not only escaped judgment with the other inhabitants of Jericho, she was engrafted into the blessings of Abraham, and like Ruth after her, conceived seed in her womb that brought forth the promise.

Application

Following Rahab and Ruth's example in applying the blood of the cross to our hearts, we are no longer condemned. The witnesses of our head and heart are also poised, like those at the gate of Jerusalem, waiting to pronounce the blessing of Abraham on the seed of God's word in our hearts. All we have to do is conceive it.

In order to bring focus to the plethora of possibilities available in Abraham's blessing, let's look at one verse. In changing Abram's name to Abraham, consider that God pronounced the following blessing on him, *"And I will make you exceeding fruitful, and I will make nations of you, and kings shall come out of you"* (Genesis 17:6).

If we take the liberty to rearrange the threefold blessing contained here, we would recognize that God has called each of us to a measure of leadership as kings. That will look different for each person. That may be at home, work, school, at church, or on a grander scale in leading a city or country. Basically, wherever others are gathered behind you becomes your nation or clan. The final stanza in this blessing is one of seeing the promises of God birthed through you. So, Abraham's blessing means you are a king, people will gather behind you and there will be a resultant fruitfulness (king > nation > fruitfulness). Take the time to meditate and imagine what this threefold blessing looks like for you.

Chapter 25

JACOB'S ENTRY AND EXIT

Genesis 28:1-22; 32:22-31

And He said unto him, "Truly, truly, I say unto you,
Hereafter you shall see heaven open, and the angels of God
ascending and descending upon the Son of Man" (John 1:51).

Having considered that Jesus' declaration to Nathaniel of angels ascending and descending on the Son of Man, disclosed something of their work. We now move to the revealing of a deeper truth hidden in the incident.

In referencing a scene played out in the life of Jacob, Jesus is identifying Himself with Jacob and linking the two. The connection is strengthened by Jesus' use of key words in recognizing that Nathaniel was *"an Israelite, indeed, in whom is no deceit!"* (John 1:47). This is because Jacob, who dreamed of angels ascending and descending, left Canaan as a man in whom was guile, but returned with a new name, Israel, a prince with God: a man with no deceit.

Jacob's Exit and Entry

Jacob's journey from Canaan to Haran to find a wife (Genesis 28:1-2) is a picture of Jesus' departure from heaven to earth to woo His bride. This is in part depicted in Jacob leaving Beersheba to go to Haran. Beersheba means Well of the Seven, while Haran carries the thought of a parched land. Jacob's dream of angels ascending and descending equates with Jesus' exit from heaven and entry to earth, while His re-entry to heaven is found in Jacob's wrestle with God at Peniel. Hence, in using the title Son of Man, Jesus was making reference to His taking on humanity; and Jacob's renaming to become Israel at Peniel, points to Jesus returning as the Son of God.

From Entry to Exit

When Jesus spoke to Nathaniel, there was no mention of the ladder featured in Jacob's dream because the angels were ascending and descending on the Son of Man. Both scenes are pictures of Jesus on the cross, hanging between heaven and earth. That's right. Jesus started His earthly ministry with an eternal perspective; and even though the cross hadn't yet taken place chronologically, the Lamb was already slain in heaven.

Though it may be difficult to comprehend, in the Spirit Jesus entered and exited earth on the cross. In other words, Jesus was a dead man walking during His earthly ministry, which is demonstrated all the way from His baptism through to His vicarious sacrifice on the cross. Thus we read:

> ...when He comes into the world, he says, Sacrifice and offering you would not, but a body You have prepared for me (Hebrews 10:5).

Even as the Son of man came not to be ministered unto, but to minister, and to give his life a ransom for many (Matthew 20:28).

This understanding provides much-needed insight into the true cost of discipleship because a call to follow Jesus is a call to be a living sacrifice (Romans 12:1). This truth is reiterated by Jesus Himself as He prefaces His call for followers to first take up their cross in order to qualify:

And he that takes not his cross, and follows after me, is not worthy of me. He that finds his life shall lose it: and he that loses his life for my sake shall find it (Matthew 10:38-39).

...If any man will come after me, let him deny himself, and take up his cross, and follow me. For whosoever will save his life shall lose it: and whosoever will lose his life for my sake shall find it (Matthew 16:24-25).

This is in keeping with the thought that followers emulate the one they are following. By repeating Himself, Jesus removed any likelihood that His words could be understood to be contextually scripted, to apply only to a certain stratum or subculture in society. He was addressing all His followers. It was to this same group of people that John the apostle was speaking when he said, *"He that says he abides in him ought himself also so to walk, even as he walked"* (1 John 2:6).

Jacob's Exit

It is no coincidence that in crossing the ford at the brook (a Hebrew male noun) at Jabbok (meaning emptying itself), that we encounter Jacob alone, pouring himself out as he wrestles with God. The scene echoes what would later be played out in the Garden of Gethsemane. Like Jacob who prevailed against God and man, Jesus overcame men in their attempts to bind Him in His words (Matthew 22:15-22; 23-33;34-46) and clung to the cup of suffering from His Father, in spite of the pain (Matthew 20:22; 26:39,42).

The hollow of Jacob's hip out of joint symbolizes Jesus' heart experiencing total rejection. During this encounter, Jacob underwent a name change. He went from being Jacob, meaning supplanter, grabber, to Israel, meaning prince with God. Jesus, who took on being *Son of Man,* was from this point recognized as the *Son of God.* For Jacob, the transformation was complete, just as the new day was breaking while for Christ, in returning to His former glory, the Sun was rising (Malachi 4:2).

There is one key element in the episode at Peniel that is revealed, and yet remains hidden. Before Jacob received a blessing, he asked God His name. There was no audible reply, and yet there was a reply. The blessing he received telegraphed the reply. Why didn't God openly reply? He didn't reply, because the answer was "a given." Who imparts a blessing? Jacob already knew the answer. A father imparts the blessing; after all. that's who Jacob had deceived to steal his brother's blessing. When God doesn't respond audibly to Jacob but imparts a blessing anyway, He is saying, I am Father.

Jesus, in speaking to the disciples on that fateful night that traversed into Gethsemane, introduced them to the Father in His intercessory prayer, which began, *"Father, the hour is come; glorify Your Son..."* (John 17:1-26). A father blesses his children. Jesus has reintroduced us to the Father. Jacob was transformed from having to steal a blessing from his earthly father, to openly receiving a blessing from his heavenly Father.

Entry through the Cross

Given this discussion of Christ as a dead man walking, it needs to be said that Jesus is not still on the cross. However, the eternal nature of that one-time event means we are able to access its provision endlessly. In short, He is the door and His death opened heaven to us. The charge of humanity's sin upheld by the angel with the flaming sword, the word of judgment, keeping humankind barred from God's garden has been dropped, because justice has been met through the blood of His Son. Like Jacob, Adam stole to receive a perceived fruitful blessing and was cast out because of it—while the last Adam, Jesus, wrestled on our behalf to bring us home again to our Father.

Application

The first place we are living sacrifices is before Him in prayer. Take the time to offer yourself to Him privately, today.

Jacob received a two-pronged blessing from his earthly father, Isaac. His father first spoke of the dew of heaven and then the fruit of the earth. First heaven, then earth. First spirit, then natural. If you are a parent, natural or spiritual, prepare and speak a twofold blessing over your children.

Chapter 26

LABAN AND THE LAW

Genesis 29:1–31:54

Having pegged the commencement and end of Jacob's journey as a parallel of Christ's mission to earth, it is time to consider what took place while he was in Haran. What is hidden beneath the narrative—featuring Laban, Leah, and Rachel, together with the spotted and speckled flocks and herds—strengthens our understanding of the gospel.

The Stone Over the Well

When Jacob arrived in Haran, the shepherds were waiting for the authorities to roll the stone off the well's mouth so they could water their flocks. The scene depicts the priesthood restricting the flow of the Spirit through the Law etched in stone. Jesus is seen rolling away the word of condemnation and releasing life-giving words to His hearers, as Jacob removes the stone to water Rachel's flock (Genesis 29:6-10).

Jacob's Two Wives

Jacob is taken into Laban's household where he serves his host to gain the hand of his two daughters, Leah and Rachel, in marriage. This immediately raises questions in relation to Jesus' marriage to the Church. How is it that Jacob marries two wives, and yet Christ has one?

In order to understand this apparent anomaly, we need to overview the storyline and identify the characters. Working under Laban's authority, Jacob serves for fourteen years to earn the hand of his wives. The plot is a little convoluted because Jacob, who was in love with Rachel, had to first marry her sister, Leah, before he could be united with the one he loved.

Keys are released throughout the narrative to help us identify the characters in this drama. The first of these is found when Jacob prepared his wives to leave their father and make the journey home with him. At that time, he said that Laban had *"deceived me and changed my wages ten times"* (Genesis 31:7,41). Here, the Holy Spirit is alluding to the law, which comprises of ten commandments, that when broken produce *"the wages of sin"* (Romans 6:23). Thus, when Jacob spoke of being *deceived* by Laban, he is in harmony with the apostle Paul who writes:

> *And the commandment, which was ordained to life, I found to be unto death. For sin, taking occasion by the commandment, deceived me, and by it slew me* (Romans 7:10-11).

Further to this, the word used by Jacob when he said Laban *changed* my wages, has multiple meanings. While it does mean to change, it also means to pierce through and to pass away. So while on one level it described Laban's personal underhanded shenanigans, on another plane the verse also describes the deadly power of the law (Romans 7:11). This is why it is recorded, that God warned Laban later in a dream *"not to speak either good or bad"* to Jacob (Genesis 31:24).

It does so because Jesus was sinless and could not be accused according to the law. It had no power to add to Him, neither could it hold Him to account. Therefore, Laban is a depiction of the law. Jacob bringing his wives out of Haran is a picture of God's Son being sent forth to redeem those being *"kept under the law"* (Galatians 3:23; 4:4-5). Rachel and Leah's acceptance of Jacob's directive to leave the place depicts them as those *"led by the Spirit"* and no longer *"under the law"* (Galatians 5:18).

In considering Jacob's two wives. Leah is described as being *"tender eyed,"* while Rachel is the more visually attractive of the two sisters. Leah is a picture of the nation of Israel, locked up in the law without the ability to see her Messiah and act in faith. Rachel represents the Gentile world, who, like the woman at the well, the centurion, and the Syrophoenician woman, perceived who Jesus was and demonstrated great faith. Just as the gospel had to first be preached to the Jews before being sent abroad among the Gentiles, Jacob had first to marry Leah (Romans 1:16). In the same way that Jacob's love for Rachel stirred Leah into seeking greater intimacy (Genesis 30:9-21), in like manner, the Gentile church will stir the Jews to jealousy (Romans 10:19; 11:11). However, unlike Jacob's individual marriages to Rachel and Leah, *"God so loved the world..."* means that God's eyes were always on the bigger prize, incorporating both Jew and Gentile, in one bride.

The Spotted and Speckled

Though many obscure sermons have been construed to fit Jacob's visual display before the watering troughs, the spiritual overlay is much less fabricated and simply profound. The Bible records:

> *Now Jacob took for himself rods of green poplar and of the almond and chestnut trees, peeled white strips in them, and exposed the white which was in the rods. And the rods which he had peeled, he set before the flocks in the gutters,*

in the watering troughs where the flocks came to drink, so that they should conceive when they came to drink. So the flocks conceived before the rods, and the flocks brought forth streaked, speckled, and spotted (Genesis 30:37-39 NKJV).

The rod is a picture of the shepherd's staff, which conveys the authority and protection of the word of God (Genesis 32:10; Psalm 23:4; Exodus 14:16; Hebrews 4:12). To peel back the bark so as to expose the white cambium layer beneath is a picture of removing the jacket or covering of the word of God to release life-giving revelation that would otherwise remain hidden. The watering troughs are a picture of people's hearts, which on receiving revelation conceive the promises of God. The different trees represent the depth and variety within the word from which His promises are found. While the bringing forth of streaked, spotted, and speckled speaks of the humble and ignoble hearers who bring forth fruit.

Application

Pray for Israel, that the religious covering would be stripped away, that the revelation of the waters of life would be received into Jewish hearts.

What part does humility play in receiving from God?

The centurion who sought Jesus for the healing of his servant was a man of authority. What do you think may have humbled him to receive from Christ?

Chapter 27

JONAH

Jonah 1:1-17

Jesus and Jonah

When Jesus made an association between Himself and Jonah, He gave us the green light to look more closely at Jonah's story. There were many times when the scribes and Pharisees asked for a sign from Him (Matthew 16:1; Mark 8:11; Luke 11:16; John 2:18; 6:30). On this occasion, He responded, by saying:

> *An evil and adulterous generation seeks after a sign; and there shall no sign be given to it, but the sign of the prophet Jonah: For as Jonah was three days and three nights in the whale's belly; so shall the Son of man be three days and three nights in the heart of the earth* (Matthew 12:39-40).

While Jesus was primarily speaking about His resurrection, does the parallel that exists between the two hide other insights for us? If the resurrection were our main focus, then the second chapter must of necessity be an account of Jesus' journey through hell, and its closing verse, an account of His resurrection:

> *And the Lord spoke unto the fish, and it vomited out Jonah upon the dry land* (Jonah 2:10).

Beyond the Resurrection

Now, apart from making you wonder what a resurrected person smells like, such a succinct, one-line account in a book of four chapters would suggest that there has to be more here surrounding Christ's death. So what about the rest of Jonah's story? Admittedly, there are some difficult passages to navigate in establishing the parallel between Jesus and Jonah. Especially Jonah's fleeing from God in its opening and his bouts of anger in the final chapter.

Jesus Sent to Jerusalem

Jonah's story opens with God calling him to address the wickedness of the great city of Nineveh, the capital of Assyria (Jonah 1:2). Beneath this scenario, God is doing the same to Jerusalem, who is similarly recognized as *great* in Matthew 5:35 and Revelation 11:8 and whose evil wickedness was the very reason Jesus would not perform signs for them (see Matthew 12:39).

Jonah's journey to Tarshish is the equivalent of Jesus' journey from heaven.

In the Books of Kings and Isaiah, ocean-going merchant ships are called *"ships of Tarshish,"* as a depiction of the type of vessel required to make the long voyage (1 Kings 10:22; Isaiah 23:1,14). Jesus made that voyage for us. To emphasize the point, Jonah is reported as going *down* to Joppa, *down* into the ship, *down* inside the ship, where he lay *down*. Apostle Paul relates the same, speaking of Jesus:

Who, being in the form of God, thought it not robbery to be equal with God: But made himself of no reputation, and took upon him the form of a servant, and was made in the likeness of men: And being found in fashion as a man, he humbled himself, and became obedient unto death, even the death of the cross (Philippians 2:6-8).

Jesus made the same downward journey. Now, what about the fact that it said Jonah did *"flee"* from the presence of the Lord? Again, this is no issue, as the same Hebrew word is elsewhere interpreted as passing and doing something with haste. The storm Jerusalem was experiencing, at the time of Christ, was described by John the apostle:

And when the dragon saw that he was cast unto the earth, he persecuted the woman which brought forth the man child. ...And the serpent cast out of his mouth water as a flood after the woman, that he might cause her to be carried away of the flood (Revelation 12:13,15).

The Scapegoat

In casting lots to determine who would bear the responsibility for their predicament, the sailors are, in effect, going through the motions of selecting the scapegoat (Leviticus 16:8-26). Like Jonah, the Jews asked Jesus who He was (John 10:24), and He, in like fashion, responded that He had come from the presence of the Father (John 10:36). In casting Jonah into the sea, the captain is emulating Caiaphas, who prophesied that one man should die, that the whole nation should not perish (John 11:49-52). Jesus' innocence was likewise recognized by several who found themselves awash in Roman-occupied Jerusalem at the time (Matthew 27:19,23; Luke 23:41,47; Acts 3:13).

The Sea

In Scripture, the sea is recognized as being beneath the earth (Deuteronomy 4:18), as the place of the dead (Psalm 68:22) and in its depths, the holding place for our sin (Micah 7:19). Thus, as Jonah is thrown into the sea, Jesus was killed and offered as a sacrifice, entering death for us. At that moment, like the centurion, at the foot of the cross, who had to acknowledge the hand of God at work that day (Mark 15:39), the sailors made vows in awe of the silencing of the tempestuous sea.

Some who read this may ask, "That's great, so there is this spiritual overlay present here, but where is the fruit in it?" The fruit is found in recognizing the love of God for humankind; the fruit is found in understanding beneath our everyday lives lies spiritual activity; the fruit is found acknowledging God's mastery of life on earth; the fruit is found developing a vocabulary of the spirit realm; the fruit is found in a new hunger for the word of God; and the fruit is found in beckoning His children deeper into the things of the Spirit. In fact, that is the only place fruit is found.

Application

While Jonah was in rebellion, Jesus never was.

Does Jonah increase your understanding of the spiritual climate into which Jesus came?

Like the disciples on the Emmaus Road, does your heart burn within you for more?

If you considered your life a poem or parable with the truth hidden within, what would be the theme, mission, or lessons it contains?

What part of Jonah's story does your life most closely resemble at the moment?

Jesus made reference to Jonah spending three days and three nights in the belly of the great fish. Some people struggle with the reality of such an event. Do you think the same people would be the ones who struggle with the concept of hell? Why or why not?

Chapter 28

GOING THROUGH HELL

Jonah 2:1–3:10

The Dove

Gaining an understanding of the bigger picture of the Book of Jonah, especially what is otherwise hidden beneath its narrative, helps put things in context. So to that end, the key that links all four chapters, including the demonstrative outbursts of anger in the final chapter, is the meaning of Jonah's name. Jonah means dove. The dove is the object of God's affection, it typifies Jesus' meek and gentle spirit; it is representative of the sensitivity of the Holy Spirit; and finally, it depicts Jerusalem, the choice daughter of her mother, Israel.

The Book of Jonah can be described as:

Chapter 1: Jesus' love (dove of God's love) for humanity (Song of Songs 5:2)

Chapter 2: Jesus in hell (the mournful dove) (Isaiah 38:14)

Chapter 3: Jesus and Holy Spirit in Jerusalem (John 1:32)

Chapter 4: Jerusalem's (God's dove) angry response to Jesus (Song of Songs 6:9)

That said, the first chapter of Jonah closes with a parenthesis, a bracketed summary providing the timespan of Jonah and Christ's sojourn through hell:

> *Now the Lord had prepared a great fish to swallow up Jonah. And Jonah was in the belly of the fish three days and three nights* (Jonah 1:17).

Going Through Hell

If you wanted insight into Jesus' experience in hell, then what follows this verse in the second chapter of Jonah provides one aspect of that journey, just as an understanding of a word can be more fully understood by considering its antonym, its opposite. Perhaps a true appreciation of the kingdom Jesus has won for us would be found in seeing something of the torment of its counterpart, hell. While that will not be the deliberate focus here, there are a few standout verses in the second chapter worth considering such as, *"...out of the belly of hell I cried, and You heard my voice"* (Jonah 2:2).

Having already heard from Jesus Himself, confirming His connection with Jonah, with this verse we now more openly recognize that in singing of his own deliverance, King David was prophetically revealing an eternal scene of Jesus in hell when he sang:

> *The sorrows of hell compassed me about: the snares of death prevented me. In my distress I called upon the Lord, and cried unto my God: He heard my voice out of His temple, and my cry came before Him, even into His ears* (Psalm 18:5-6).

What I love about this is both its simplicity and profundity. That no matter what it is we are going through, and no matter where we are, our Father in heaven hears our prayer. There is an assurance in knowing when we unearth our heart before Him, He is there listening and working all things together for our good. Even though at that moment, it may feel like He is a million miles away.

Hell's Separation

In fact, part of the torment of hell is the absolute sense of separation from the Father. This is why it is recorded that Jesus experienced the ultimate separation, as expressed when He cried out, *"My God, My God, why have You forsaken Me?"* (Psalm 22:1). In His going to hell, He removed the sentence that hung over our heads (Colossians 2:14), so we would no longer experience its consequences:

> *Who shall separate us from the love of Christ? ...For I am persuaded, that neither death, nor life, nor angels, nor principalities, nor powers, nor things present, nor things to come, Nor height, nor depth, nor any other creature, shall be able to separate us from the love of God, which is in Christ Jesus our Lord* (Romans 8:35-39).

What is not said in all of this, but which is provided by scenes of hell as a contrast, is that His presence is the very atmosphere and fragrance of the kingdom. For where the King is, there is the kingdom.

Thanksgiving Brought Deliverance

Finally, after they endured waves of despair, God's chastisement, and found themselves in a state of utter hopelessness, both Jonah and Jesus *"remembered"* the Lord. As they did so, their imagination was engaged until a prayer of thanksgiving bursts from their lips, and with it, deliverance came.

> *But I will sacrifice unto thee with the voice of thanksgiving;*
> *I will pay that that I have vowed. Salvation is of the Lord.*
> *And the Lord spoke unto the fish, and it vomited out—*
> *Jonah upon the dry land* (Jonah 2:9-10).

A Random Verse?

There is one other verse in the midst of Jonah's torturous experience in hell that at first seems rather randomly placed. It's the sort of verse that stands out because it doesn't seem to fit the flow of what is going on around it: *"They that observe lying vanities forsake their own mercy"* (Jonah 2:8).

This verse is deliberately placed to precede Jonah's exclamation of praise, as a point of contrast:

> *They that observe lying vanities forsake their own mercy.*
> *But I will sacrifice...with...thanksgiving* (Jonah 2:8-9).

In light of the parallel between Jonah and Jesus, why is it here, and what does it mean? It means that during Christ's sojourn in hell, He saw others in torment around Him. The reason they were there, was because they lost spiritual focus and got caught up in the froth and bubble of life around them. It is so easy to be drawn away from eternal realities when our idols are not simply cast or clay figurines on a shelf. When they are instead the superficial and transitory issues and things after which the world chases.

Chapter 3

There's hope for all of us in the opening line of Jonah's third chapter, *"And the word of the Lord came unto Jonah the second time..."* (Jonah 3:1).

Whew! We can all breathe a sigh of relief that God is the God of the second chance. In relation to Christ's ministry and what is taking place in the spirit realm, this chapter carries us into Jerusalem. Jonah records Nineveh was an exceedingly great city of three days' journey (Jonah 3:3). For Jesus, that journey was His term passing through hell. So while Jonah is physically present before the Ninevites, here we pick up the post-resurrection ministry of both Christ and the Holy Spirit. Jonah's proclamation that in forty days Nineveh will be overthrown is a parallel of Jesus releasing understanding on the kingdom:

> *To whom also he showed himself alive after his passion by many infallible proofs, being seen of them forty days, and speaking of the things pertaining to the kingdom of God* (Acts 1:3).

The Establishment of His Heavenly Kingdom

In Jonah's proclamation to Nineveh, God was announcing to Jerusalem the replacement of His expression through Israel's earthly kingdom. He was about to establish something much greater—His heavenly kingdom. Let's get it straight, the new kingdom is not limited to earthly constraints, it is inclusive of everyone who believes, including the Jews. Neither is God done with Israel because Paul assures us that though they may have been cast off, like Christ, they will rise from the dead (Romans 11:15).

The Holy Spirit at Work

The rest of the chapter is about the Holy Spirit at work, as He reproves the world of sin and of righteousness and of judgment (John 16:8). Jonah's message was heard:

So the people of Nineveh believed God, and proclaimed a fast, and put on sackcloth, from the greatest of them even to the least of them (Jonah 3:5).

The record, found inlaid within Jonah's story, suggests there was a seamless transition from Christ to the Holy Spirit, as there is no juncture in the narrative. For Jonah, the whole city repented. However, Jesus foresaw He would be rejected and the city overthrown,

The men of Nineveh shall rise in judgment with this generation, and shall condemn it: because they repented at the preaching of Jonah; and, behold, a greater than Jonah is here (Matthew 12:41).

And Jesus went out, and departed from the temple: and his disciples came to him for to show him the buildings of the temple. And Jesus said unto them, See you not all these things? Truly I say unto you, There shall not be left here one stone upon another, that shall not be thrown down (Matthew 24:1-2).

Christ's awaiting rejection was foretold, hidden within Jonah's fourth chapter.

Application

With a renewed understanding of God's ability to hear your prayer, is there anything you would like to say right now to the Father?

What part does meditation play in recognizing nothing can separate us from the love of God in Christ Jesus?

If there is anything troubling you right now, consider the bigger picture for a moment or two, and as you are able, start thanking God, knowing He has a greater plan beyond what you are going through.

Chapter 29

THE FOURTH DOVE

Jonah 4:1-11

Jerusalem

The rejection Christ was to receive was foretold in Jonah's fourth chapter. Hidden beneath the record of Jonah's tantrums was the story of another dove. It's here that Jerusalem is center stage as the choice daughter of her mother, the dove of His love:

> *My dove, my undefiled is but one; she is the only one of her mother, she is the choice one of her that bore her. The daughters saw her, and blessed her; yea, the queens and the concubines, and they praised her* (Song of Songs 6:9).

Jerusalem was chosen (2 Chronicles 6:6; Zechariah 3:2), it was Jerusalem that was the apple of God's eye (Zechariah 2:7-8), and it was to Jerusalem that the Queen of Sheba came and gave praise (2 Chronicles 9:1).

This means that beneath Jonah's anger at God's repentance to destroy Nineveh, lies the revealing of the heart of the city of Jerusalem, led by its power brokers (Matthew 15:12; 21:46; 27:18; Mark 3:6). To make matters worse, beneath Jonah's confession of the heart of God, he was also revealing knowledge held by the scribes and Pharisees:

> ...*I knew that You are a gracious God, and merciful, slow to anger, and of great kindness, and repent You of the evil* (Jonah 4:2).

Jerusalem's Rejection of Christ

It is upon this backdrop that Jonah's lack of compassion toward Nineveh depicts Jerusalem's hardness of heart toward God's love for humankind. Similar to Jonah, Jesus had been preparing Jerusalem for potential destruction. When Jonah expressed three times that he would rather die than live, it confirmed Jerusalem's rejection, first of Christ and then the Holy Spirit. It also likely assigned their fate. While we may think 3,000 souls saved on the Day of Pentecost is awesome, Josephus Hacataeus wrote in the 4th century BC that Jerusalem was inhabited by 120,000 men.[1] It is really these men who are being referred to as those unable to discern between their right and left hands in the very last verse (Jonah 4:11). This accounts for Jerusalem's destruction, and likely explains why it was 120 souls (1 in 1,000) that gave birth to the new nation-kingdom on the Day of Pentecost.

The Prophetic Object Lesson

After delivering his message, Jonah made his camp outside the city to watch what would become of it; it was here that God spoke to him through a prophetic object lesson. In that place, Jonah erected a booth, and it appears its framework became a trellis upon which a gourd was able to grow. The Bible records Jonah was grateful for the shade it provided. No sooner was Jonah enjoying his good fortune, cool in the shade, before a worm struck the gourd, and it dried up. At that point, Jonah became angry again because things weren't going as planned.

The gourd is a type of fast-growing vine and as such was a picture of Israel. Living in booths was symbolic of the transitory life Israel experienced making the journey to the Promised Land (Leviticus 23:43). The worm that struck the vine is elsewhere translated as scarlet and scarlet thread because of the dye that was produced from its larvae, and was used to color twine. The scarlet thread, as has been discussed elsewhere, represents both the blood of Christ and a breach or engrafting into the bloodline. Hence, when God confronted Jonah for his wrongful anger over his misfortune, He is actually addressing Jerusalem in their indignation over God's right to replace the vine, which He established and sustained, with a scarlet thread. In other words, the temporary and transitory nature of booth life was about to be replaced with an eternal kingdom, birthed through Christ's blood.

Jesus foresaw destruction coming to Jerusalem. Yet in His love for Israel, came to lead those with ears to hear into the new kingdom. Knowing full well that most would not accept His message, He came anyway. Like Jonah before Him, His death and resurrection was their much sought-after sign, an opportunity to avoid destruction through repentance and faith.

Application

There was a seamless transition between Christ and the Holy Spirit. Ask the Holy Spirit to lead you from the cross, deeper into the kingdom He has prepared for you.

God's prophetic object lessons are around us all the time. What has been the most recent major news headline that has caught your attention? If God were speaking through that event, what do you think He would be saying?

Those who were unable to discern between their right and left hands were those who did not know what was and what was not of God. How do pride, politics, and possessions influence a person's ability to discern what God is saying?

ENDNOTE

1. Drawing from the Diaspora—the dispersion of the Jews through Babylonian captivity—it is estimated that Jerusalem swelled to around 3,000,000 people during Passover.

Chapter 30

TWO ROCKS

Nicodemus' Visit

At one time, Jesus had a visit from a Pharisee named Nicodemus. In their conversation, while His visitor was still working on the customary preliminaries, Jesus cut straight through the small talk by going to the heart of the matter and declares:

> *Truly, truly, I say unto you, Except a man be born again, he cannot see the kingdom of God* (John 3:3).

Nicodemus was puzzled, *"How can a man be born when he is old?"* he asked. While he was trying to get his head around that one, Jesus fired another salvo:

> *Truly, truly, I say unto you, Except a man be born of water and of the Spirit, he cannot enter into the kingdom of God* (John 3:5).

These two volleys placed Nicodemus totally out of his depth and trying to find a footing to speak. So, not understanding, he asked, *"How can these things be?"* To which Jesus responded, *"Are you the teacher of Israel, and don't know these things?"* Looking at the two statements Jesus made, notice that one of the truths He revealed spoke of seeing and the other of entering. Jesus acknowledged Nicodemus as *the* teacher of Israel, and yet he didn't know these things. He was not only pointing out that you can teach God's word for years and still miss the truth it contains, He was also alluding to something deeper.

Nicodemus was struggling to understand Jesus' saying at its simplest level. The surface meaning of Jesus' riddle was that just as people are born naturally, they also need their Father in heaven to open their spiritual eyes to see heavenly realities. In other words, they first need a spiritual birth. However, Jesus was actually speaking on a deeper level; but because Nicodemus had trouble grasping its simplest application, He added:

> *If I have told you earthly things, and you believe not, how shall you believe, if I tell you of heavenly things?* (John 3:12)

Nicodemus didn't even understand the basic meaning of Jesus' teaching. If he had, like many veiled to the kingdom, he would probably have been content with that. In this last comment, Jesus deliberately referred to something beyond the earthly application, knowing it would open within His visitor a desire and hunger for more.

As a teacher of Israel's sacred writings, his taste buds now prepared, Jesus knew that when Nicodemus left Him, he would come to recognize that Jesus was alluding to Moses. It was Moses, who saw but was unable to enter the Promised Land (Numbers 20:12; 27:12). Moses' life example teaches that it is one thing to see the kingdom, and quite another to enter.

Moses and the Two Rocks

Looking back at what happened to Moses, there were two marked occasions in Israel's wilderness wanderings when the people complained to Moses about the lack of water. One is found early, and the other late in their journey to the Promised Land. When instructing Moses at the first, God said:

> ...*Go on before the people, and take with you of the elders of Israel; and your rod, wherewith you smote the river, take in your hand, and go. Behold, I will stand before you there upon the rock in Horeb; and you shall smite the rock, and there shall come water out of it, that the people may drink. And Moses did so in the sight of the elders of Israel* (Exodus 17:5-6).

The scene before us is one of Jesus on the cross. When Moses struck the rock, he was striking Jesus, who was standing upon the rock, as the rock of our salvation (Psalm 89:26). The act of striking is a picture of the judgment Jesus received on the cross (Exodus 12:12; Isaiah 5:25). It is significant that it was Moses, the law-giver, who was the arm of judgment here. The water pouring forth from the rock portrays God's life-giving deliverance and provision through it.

The second rock occurrence was late in Israel's journey. At that time, God's instruction to Moses was:

> *Take the rod, and gather you the assembly together, you, and Aaron your brother, and speak you unto the rock before their eyes; and it shall give forth his water, and you shall bring forth to them water out of the rock: so you shall give the congregation and their animals drink* (Numbers 20:8).

However, the event went down somewhat differently:

> *Moses and Aaron gathered the congregation together before the rock, and he said unto them, Hear now, you rebels; must we fetch you water out of this rock? And Moses lifted up his hand, and with his rod he smote the rock twice: and the*

water came out abundantly, and the congregation drank, and their animals also (Numbers 20:10-11).

A Fatal Error

Moses was instructed to speak to the rock, and yet here we read he struck it again, and this time, twice. If the first rock incident represented the judgment of Jesus upon the cross, then in striking the rock again, Moses was, in effect, re-crucifying Christ. His failure to move on with the Living God meant he was unable to enter the promised kingdom. Pretty simple really. That said, it appeared the root of the problem lay in what preceded him striking the rock. Moses made a fatal error by drawing glory to himself. Even though he may have tried to camouflage his self-aggrandizement by including his brother Aaron in his address to Israel, God identified the issue when He said:

> ...*Because you believed* [established] *Me not, to sanctify me* [set apart as holy] *in the eyes of the children of Israel, therefore you shall not bring this congregation into the land which I have given them* (Numbers 20:12).

Give God the Glory

In this rebuke, God explained that in not elevating and setting Him apart as the One who is enthroned in heaven, sanctifying Him, Moses had inadvertently failed to establish the kingdom over which God reigns. How did he do that? Well, God's instruction for Moses to speak to the rock was an invitation to exercise kingdom authority as a prince seated with Him in heavenly places. He was meant to demonstrate kingdom life to us as heirs of God by speaking the revelatory word.

However, in drawing glory to himself and looking to revisit old manna, he dethroned God and effectively re-crucified Christ. As a consequence, there was no kingdom to enter. Did water flow from the rock? Absolutely! It did so because of God's grace and love for those under Moses' leadership.

Just as Moses crossed the Red Sea (water) but fell short of traversing the Jordan River (Spirit), there are those who are born again but similarly fail to enter the eternal kingdom. It is not a given that once you are born again you automatically enter the kingdom He has prepared for us. Moses did not follow the revelation given him and he drew attention to himself when he was before the people. These are two very important mistakes to avoid—young and old alike.

Application

In any narrative or historical setting, both in life and in Scripture, there is earthly wisdom that can be gained and a deeper heavenly truth to be revealed. What are your latest godly insights at either level?

Why is it important that God gets the glory before entry to His kingdom and its provision become manifest?

What rocks in front of you need to give forth their water? Has God given you a revelatory word to speak, that they give up their provision?

Is it possible that those who dwell at the cross may be guilty of re-crucifying Christ, and like Moses, are unable to enter as a consequence?

Chapter 31

THE CROSS AS A TREE

So having discussed that man, in some contexts, may metaphorically be represented as a tree, did you ever notice that the New Testament makes reference to the cross as a tree? Hence, we read:

> *The God of our fathers raised up Jesus, whom you slew and hanged on a tree* (Acts 5:30).

> *And we are witnesses of all things which He did both in the land of the Jews, and in Jerusalem; whom they slew and hanged on a tree* (Acts 10:39).

> *And when they had fulfilled all that was written of Him, they took Him down from the tree, and laid Him in a sepulchre* (Acts 13:29).

> *Christ has redeemed us from the curse of the law, having become a curse for us (for it is written, "Cursed is everyone who hangs on a tree")* (Galatians 3:13 NKJV).

> *Who Himself bore our sins in His own body on the tree...* (1 Peter 2:24 NKJV).

Bitter Waters

However, this symbolism is not exclusive to the New Testament and so we also find the cross represented by a tree, as the central element, when Moses was instructed how to make bitter waters sweet (Exodus 15:23-26).

> *So Moses brought Israel from the Red Sea, and they went out into the wilderness of Shur; and they went three days in the wilderness, and found no water. And when they came to Marah, they could not drink of the waters of Marah, for they were bitter: therefore the name of it was called Marah. And the people murmured against Moses, saying, What shall we drink? And he cried unto the Lord; and the Lord showed him a tree, which when he had cast into the waters, the waters were made sweet: there he made for them a statute and an ordinance, and there he proved them, And said, If you will diligently hearken to the voice of the Lord your God, and will do that which is right in his sight, and will give ear to his commandments, and keep all his statutes, I will put none of these diseases upon you, which I have brought upon the Egyptians: for am the Lord that heals you* (Exodus 15:22-26).

In brief, the bitter waters of Marah are a picture of the bitterness, complaint, and hostility that pours forth from the human heart. While the tree that was cast into the water depicts the cross applied to the depth of humanity's heart to change, as it were, the very nature of a person's DNA.

The incident at Marah was so prominent in the heart of God that it was marked by Him with a decree, a statute, a legal judgment, an ordinance, and a promise. If Israel would diligently heed the voice of God,

His *rhema* word, and do what was commanded, God would not allow the sickness and diseases that plagued the world to come upon them.

Changes to DNA?

Though we may want to question the validity of changes to a person's DNA, the Scriptures, on the other hand, declare:

> *Therefore, if anyone is in Christ, he is a new creature; old things have passed away; behold all things have become new* (2 Corinthians 5:17).

This new creature, according to the Greek, is something that has never been seen before. This is a newly introduced species, the first appearing of the amalgamation of God in humans. On this point, it could be argued that Jesus' words, *"It is finished!"* mark more than just the end to the sacrificial requirements of the law, that they equally declare the completion of God's creation. Therefore, the cross marks both the death of the law and the birthing of the new creation. This is surely a masterstroke worthy of further consideration.

On the subject of DNA, a study conducted in 2012 found that female brains harbor the presence of male DNA that did not originate in the individual.[1] The male microchimerism (DNA) was obviously genetically distinct from the cells that made up the rest of the woman. Researchers established that this foreign DNA had been introduced through sexual intercourse (in some subjects more than 50 years earlier), which then entered the bloodstream and collected in the brain and spine.

Admittedly, this raises a number of other interesting lines of thought. In relation to the new creation, the point is that if DNA is transferred from one individual to another through sexual union, and given the physical is really but a shadow of what supersedes this realm—the spirit realm—how much more should we apprehend the power of His union with us and our change into His likeness?

The Legal Decree Associated with the Cross

The cross is the ultimate fulfillment of the drama played out at Mara, in the wilderness of Shur. Therefore, we are assured that God Himself has spoken and made a legal pronouncement, nullifying any spiritual legal right for sickness and disease to beset us as His new creation. Without stirring up condemnation and guilt, could the Body of Christ experience the same mortality rate as the world around us because of our blasé attitude to the importance of revelation, ignorance of the eternal nature of the kingdom, and a lack of using our imagination when it comes to the multifaceted provision in the cross?

Drinking from Your Own Well

Another key truth revealed at Marah is succinctly caught for us in the wisdom of Solomon, when he writes:

> A wholesome [calm and healing] tongue is a tree of life,
> but perverseness [deceitfulness] in it breaks the spirit
> (Proverbs 15:4 NKJV)

Having just come out of Egypt, the Israelites were still prone to default to the language of those with whom they had grown. This is what God was addressing in this object lesson. The contrast provided by God's promise over sickness and the imagery of bitterness carried in the heart of the children of Israel points to a correlation between the two. Therefore, Israel's murmuring on encountering the bitter waters of Marah was not merely a reaction to hardship, it was a poetic enactment revealing the consequences of drinking from the poisonous waters of their own well!

Thus, Solomon says sickness readily has an entry point through words. The example at Marah and the wisdom of Solomon warn that unresolved bitterness is the cause of much sickness and disease. Therefore, it behooves us to keep clean hearts before God and speak wisely to ourselves and others because the shape, development, and fruitfulness of the trees of people's lives depend on it.

Application

God's promise of freedom from *none of these diseases* means there is provision in the cross to heal every one of the world's sicknesses and diseases! That's worth your meditation and thanksgiving.

- Get yourself the bread and wine of communion.
- Take communion—cracker or bread and a sip of the fruit of a vine.
- As you do, imagine the bread quelling any ache in your heart.
- Imagine the blood is absorbed and co-mingling with your blood, where it becomes resident DNA in you.
- Decree over your body God's promise that none of these diseases have a legal right in your body.
- Identify any words of bitterness, complaint, and hostility that have passed through your lips.
- Pray that any breach be closed through the precious blood of Christ.

ENDNOTE

1. William F.N. Chan, et al., "Male Microchimerism in the Human Female Brain"; September 26, 2012; http://journals.plos.org/plosone/article?id=10.1371/journal.pone.0045592; accessed June 15, 2018.

Chapter 32

A FIERY SERPENT

Numbers 21:4-9

And they journeyed from mount Hor by the way of the Red Sea, to compass—the land of Edom: and the soul of the people was much discouraged because of the way.

And the people spoke against God, and against Moses, Why have you brought us up out of Egypt to die in the wilderness? for there is no bread, neither is there any water; and our soul loathes this light bread.

And the Lord sent fiery serpents among the people, and they bit the people; and much people of Israel died.

Therefore the people came to Moses, and said, We have sinned, for we have spoken against the Lord, and against you; pray unto the Lord, that he take away the serpents from us. And Moses prayed for the people.

And the Lord said unto Moses, Make you a fiery serpent, and set it upon a pole: and it shall come to pass, that every one that is bitten, when he looks upon it, shall live.

And Moses made a serpent of brass, and put it upon a pole, and it came to pass, that if a serpent had bitten any man, when he beheld the serpent of brass, he lived (Numbers 21:4-9).

An easily recognizable Old Testament passage, with a cross of Christ undercurrent, is the incident where God had Moses place a brazen serpent upon a pole. The glaringly obvious correlation with its New Testament counterpart says it is a passage with incredible significance for those entering the kingdom. In short, this story furnishes hidden insights as to why some are not experiencing the kingdom financial and physical fullness they seek. It may also identify people who *"...are destroyed for lack of knowledge"* (Hosea 4:6).

The opening scene is one of people who became impatient and discouraged because of the trials they endured along the way to their Promised Land (Numbers 21:4). I'm sure we can agree that keeping one's eyes on an invisible spiritual reality, when earth seems to be shouting the opposite, is not easy. However, in becoming disgruntled, they sought to blame those they held responsible for their plight. While it is not wrong to desire the fundamentals of human nutrition, we get the feeling that their complaints about the lack of bread and water were really an expression of frustration at having not yet come to a place of fruitful rest. The people's complete disdain for manna conveys that they were still governed by the dictates of the world, rather than living by faith in the promises of God.

What happens next is the crux of the story. The Bible records that God *"sent"* fiery serpents that bit the people and many died. The word "sent" in Hebrew is *salah* (שָׁלַח). While it does mean to send forth, send away, to let go, this word also holds a secret hidden within. The letters that make up *salah* are *sheen, lamed, chet,* which also together spell out "destroy the wall of authority."

Breaking Through a Wall

What this suggests is that unrecognized by Israel as God's chosen people, they were protected and hedged about (Job 1:10; Psalm 80:12; Isaiah 5:5; Matthew 21:33). However, in criticizing and complaining, Israel's tongues created holes in the walls of the spiritual fortress that surrounded them. This was fuel for the enemy, as the accuser of the brethren, exercising his legal right. Solomon could not have captured this spiritual principle any better when he said, *"He who breaks through a wall, will be bitten by a snake"* (Ecclesiastes 10:8). James helps us understand further that in eternity, judgment is always befitting the crime when he writes, *"the tongue is an unruly evil, full of deadly poison"* (James 3:8). Jesus shows its relevance today, when He said, *"Judge not, that you not be judged"* (Matthew 7:1).

In this scene, the snakes were described as *"fiery serpents,"* a delineation that captures the painful burning sensation their victims felt after being bitten. There is an engaging and highly significant overlay that helps us broaden our understanding of the scene's relevance for application today. The words "bit" and "bitten" (Hebrew: *nasak*) are homographs, that is a word with more than one meaning. The two lines of thought this word carries are to bite and to lend or borrow with interest. Negative words are not harmless; they infect other people and have the potential to open the door to life-threatening physical problems. Many believers have been bitten or burned financially. Could it be that those who have gone through such a painful experience did so because of a spiritual law undergirding life in the natural?

Standing in the Gap

In this narrative, the people asked that Moses would pray for the removal of the snakes. Just as Moses stood in the gap—the gap the people had created—and interceded for them, in like fashion, Jesus on the cross cried to the Father, *"Forgive them for they know not what they do!"* (Luke 23:34). No wonder, Moses said God would send a Prophet like him to Israel (Deuteronomy 18:15).

The story continued with the instruction that once lifted up, if those who had been bitten looked upon the serpent, they would live. For us, this Old Testament parallel not only provides an alternative view of the cross, in adding another spiritual layer to that scene, it also provides a focus for personal application. So that in contritely beholding and heartfully considering Jesus upon the cross—the object of our judgment—Jesus' prayer of forgiveness, *"Father forgive them for they know not what they do,"* is the guarantee of an assured acquittal. What do we as onlookers have to see? The story of the brazen serpent tells us we need to consider there are spiritual consequences to criticism of leadership that seriously impact our lives.

As redeemed individuals, you and I have a hedge of protection around our lives—a boundary of blood—that the enemy cannot cross. However, we may ignorantly open fissures in that spiritual force field by the use of poisonous words that the enemy can exploit. Therefore, moving forward into the kingdom, there's a need to continually check our tongues at the door, that we give the enemy no legal grounds to beset us and intercept God's inheritance (Ephesians 4:27).

Remember, it is those *"who through faith and patience inherit the promises"* (Hebrews 6:12).

When it comes to asking forgiveness, we need to acknowledge our responsibility in controlling the tongue, make confession for what we have said, and finally, appreciate something of the enormity of the love of God and the price paid for Jesus to stand in the gap.

Application

Prayer of Repentance

Isaiah's confession: "I am a man of unclean lips...."

Repent of negativity—negativity is ultimately saying God is not good, not a Provider, not meeting my needs.

Repent for saying wrong things about leadership in the church, it says God made a wrong choice.

Ask forgiveness for infecting others with your negativity.

Ask God to restore the provision the enemy has stolen.

Ask the Lord to have the enemy release everything he has been holding back of God's bountiful provision.

Ask God to restore any health issues the enemy has afflicted.

Ask God to seal His hedge of protection around your life, in the precious blood of Jesus.

...Let a coal from the altar touch and purge my lips.

Finally, thank Him for His unfailing love and the price paid.

Chapter 33

MOSES' ROD AND HAND

Exodus 4:1-17

After the Encounter

After Moses' initial encounter with God at the burning bush, he was commanded to go and tell the elders of Israel of their meeting. As Moses was apprehensive of Israel's response to the message he was to carry, God gave him two signs to perform before his countrymen. The signs were to attest that Moses had indeed met with the Lord God of their fathers— the God of Abraham, the God of Isaac, and the God of Jacob. The signs, were further to confirm that God had witnessed their affliction under the hands of the Egyptians, and was about to bring them out unto a land flowing with milk and honey (Exodus 3:15-17).

The Message in the First Sign

As Moses struggled with God's command, he was told to cast the rod he held in his hand to the ground. As he did so, the rod became a serpent, from which he fled. The Lord told him to grab hold of the snake's tail, and as he did it became the rod again in his hand (Exodus 4:2-4). The rod in Moses hand that was cast to the ground symbolizes the Word of God, the rod in heaven coming to earth. In becoming a snake, the rod depicts the Word of God becoming the curse of sin for us (Genesis 3:14).

In grasping the snake by the tail, whereupon it once again became the rod, signifies the return of Christ to heaven where He is now ruling His kingdom through His word (Revelation 19:13-16). Christ's entry to earth, His death and ascension are to attest to the fact that God has visited His people, died upon a Roman cross, and has returned to rule from heaven (Exodus 4:5).

The Message in the Second Sign

The second sign Moses was to perform involved placing his hand into the upper part of his garment and then withdrawing it. When He did so, his hand became *"leprous as snow"* (Exodus 4:6). We can only imagine the shock and trepidation Moses must have felt on seeing his hand turn leprous. As humanity is depicted in Scripture as earthen vessels (Judges 7:16; Jeremiah 18:3-6; 2 Corinthians 4:7), the thrusting of Moses' hand beneath his garments represented the right hand of God entering the center of the earth. Turning Moses' hand leprous is a picture of God's Son taking on sin for us and entering hell (Ezekiel 32:18,24).

Two Heavenly Beings

How does leprosy represent sin? In the Book of Leviticus, the offering for the cleansing of a leper requires the presentation of two living birds to the priest. The priest commands that one of the birds is placed in an earthen vessel and killed, whereupon cedar wood, scarlet, and hyssop are dipped in the blood and then sprinkled seven times over the person who is cleansed (Leviticus 14:4-7). The other bird, which is similarly dipped in the blood is released. The range of plants selected represent the greatest, cedar, to the smallest, hyssop, and signify the range of people rich to poor, famous to insignificant for whom the cleansing applies. The two birds are two heavenly beings: Jesus, who was clothed in humanity, and killed; the other bird is the Holy Spirit who spreads the news of His cleansing throughout the world.

Resurrection Follows Death

Completing the second sign involved Moses putting his hand into his upper garment again, but this time when he withdrew it, the skin of his hand was restored to normal. Just as the first enactment represented Jesus taking our sin to hell, the second is a depiction of His resurrection, hell unable to hold Him. Hopefully you can see that the two actions—the first leprous and the second clean—are pictures of the death and resurrection of Christ.

In summary, the first sign God gave Moses to perform before the elders of Israel marked Jesus coming to earth and taking on the curse of sin for us and returning to heaven, where He now rules and reigns. His second miracle tells of Jesus as God's right hand, dying and taking our sin to hell where it is deposited before He rises triumphantly with humankind now clean from the plague of sin.

In the broader light of this discussion, how absolutely appropriate it is that the effective commencement of Jesus' ministry in the Book of Matthew is marked by the ritual of the cleansing of a leper. After He had delivered the Magna Carta on the kingdom—the Sermon on the Mount—Jesus not only announced the arrival of the two true heavenly beings and the ultimate fulfillment of leper cleansing, when you think about it, He was also foretelling the end from the beginning (Matthew 8:1-4).

Water to Blood

If Israel failed to believe the two signs and Moses' testimony, God instructed him to pour water on dry ground, whereupon the water would become blood (Exodus 4:9). Water to blood in Scripture signifies an offering and subsequent judgment (2 Kings 3:22; 2 Samuel 23:16-17; John 19:34). All those who have come to the cross have already passed through that judgment, while it still awaits those who reject it.

Breaking a Lack of Confidence

Following this narrative that opens some dimensional aspects of Christ's death upon the cross, the interaction that next takes place reveals a critical element for those journeying to and through the kingdom. It is apparent that even after God had performed multiple signs for Moses to convince his countrymen of his encounter, he still lacked confidence to complete the task he was given. And even though he was commissioned to be the vehicle for supernatural manifestations before Israel, in raising his inability to speak, Moses exposed a heart that limited God. The Lord's response provides a major key for believers to step beyond themselves and see God *do exceeding abundantly above all that we ask or think, according to the power that works in us* (Ephesians 3:20).

Tongues and Interpretation

In bringing Aaron to assist and speak on behalf of Moses, God was not only supporting him, He was also prefiguring tongues and interpretation, in Moses' stammer and Aaron's relaying of his message. While the two gifts may be seen here underlying the ministry of these two separate individuals, Moses and Aaron, the complementary expression of both gifts is not restricted by the lack of another person. This is because Moses also represents the spirit of man, while Aaron is a picture of the mouth and soul of a person.

As we move forward, what this means is, after the cross, the opening of the wells of heaven involves the release of *"rivers of living water"* (John 7:37-38). These come through the well of the believer in tongues, which is subsequently followed by an understandable expression of what God is bringing forth from heaven. That combination may be seen, as in our previous narrative, as God and His prophet (Exodus 7:1) and tongues and interpretation using two separate individuals. It may also be experienced as tongues and the expression of revelation through the same individual.

It is sad that this latter exercise of tongues, and the subsequent release of the revelatory mysteries of heaven, is overlooked by many. It appears that while we openly acknowledge the apostle Paul's contribution to the New Testament, we somehow fail to recognize the connection this has with his confession to the Corinthian church—that he spoke in tongues more than them all (1 Corinthians 14:18). One of the reasons, we fail to see the relationship between the two is because of the delay between cause and effect, especially in our "instant" modern society. Sometimes there is a delay in the release of revelation to our expression or request in tongues.

Application

Has God ever spoken to you through prophetic enactments or natural phenomena? How?

If you have a need or request of God, pray in tongues expecting a release of revelation. Understand that it may not be an instant response.

Chapter 34

ZEPHANIAH

The Lord your God in the midst of you is mighty; he will save, he will rejoice over you with joy; he will rest in his love, he will joy over you with singing (Zephaniah 3:17).

Reading, in Light of the Cross

Having repeatedly seen, how both, Old Testament and Gospel narratives are able to keep kingdom realities, hidden in plain sight, It is time, to recognize how the good news of the gospel is infused throughout Scripture, by looking at it in one verse.

> *The Lord your God in the midst* [1] *of you is mighty*[2]*; he will save* [3]*, he will rejoice* [4] *over you with joy* [5]*; he will rest* [6] *in his love* [7]*, he will joy* [8] *over you with singing* [9] (Zephaniah 3:17, numbers added).

The first thing that makes this verse from Zephaniah stand out as holding potential kingdom insight is the phrase, *"He will save."* After that has gained your attention, as you read the verse it goes on to say, *"He will rest in his love."* Who is resting? In whose love is he resting? Is this the same person resting in his own love? Or are two people involved here? While you are thinking that through and asking God whether this could prefigure the cross, a little contextual research is required. Where and to whom were these words originally spoken?

Zephaniah was a prophet during the reign of Josiah. He prophesied doom to idolatrous priests and pagan worshippers in Jerusalem. He also spoke of judgment upon the nations beyond Judah before he closed by prophesying hope, in pronouncing a remnant will be saved in Jerusalem. Verse 17 is part of that future encouragement. Though Zephaniah is directing his speech to Jerusalem, because it is also the site of Christ's passion, his words of justice and comfort have to have their ultimate fulfillment in the cross. Therefore, it looks like we can comfortably interpret this verse in light of the cross.

Going Deeper

Going deeper, beyond a surface reading, requires looking up the Hebrew words numbered 1-9 in the verse. When this is done, there is a hidden progression in the Hebrew words "rejoice"[4] and "joy"[5,8] that their generic English counterparts fail to identify. Unlike the English translation, there are three different and distinct words being used here.

Rejoice [4] sus; siys (שִׂישׂ) (שׂוּשׂ)

Joy [5] *simhah* (שִׂמְחָה)

Joy [8] *gul* (גּוּל)

Rejoice

The Hebrew word [4] used to describe rejoicing, indicates great celebration and refers to the Lord taking great delight in blessing His people. In the Book of Job, it is used in finding a cause to be happy, even over death (Job 3:22). If you are aware that the sun's arc in the sky prophetically scribes out the Messiah's mission and victory, known as the *Mazzaroth,* then its use in the psalms describing the sun rejoicing to run its race is thought-provoking (Psalm 19:5). Also note the picture created by each of the Hebrew words [4]. These depict first: His wings with a nail between them, and then, a hand between wings. Is this coincidental? Or, is it, reading too much into this? You be the judge.

Joy

The word *simhah* [5] refers to a joy and gladness associated with salvation (Psalm 51:8) and the victory in conquering one's enemies (Judges 16:23). It also used to describe the celebration of Israelite feast days (Numbers 10:10; Nehemiah 8:12; Zechariah 8:19).

The word *gul* [8] describes a joyous response. Perhaps, more to the point here, it is used to depict the rejoicing of God's people dividing the spoils of His victories (Isaiah 9:3).

Therefore, by overwriting this scene with its ultimate fulfillment at the cross, a picture of Christ is painted, spreading out His arms in anticipatory celebration of victory over the devil. This is followed by the joy of dividing the spoils of His victory with us. Is this what happened? Here, the New Testament Epistles and Book of Acts witness to our spiritual overlay. Where in speaking about Jesus, the writer to the Hebrews, says, "...*Who for the joy that was set before Him endured the cross*" (Hebrews 12:2).

And the apostle Peter, in Acts, adds:

> *For David speaks concerning him, "I foresaw the Lord always before my face, for He is on my right hand, that I should not be moved: Therefore did my heart rejoice, and my tongue was glad; moreover also my flesh shall rest in hope: Because You will not leave my soul in hell, neither will You suffer Your Holy One to see corruption* (Acts 2:25-27).

Mighty Is God in the Midst of Your Body

What really excites me about Zephaniah 3:17 is its opening line, *"The Lord your God in the midst of you is mighty."*

This is because the word "midst" [1] (Hebrew: *qereb*), especially describes all the inner organs of the body. It also represents the seat of our emotions and thoughts. This means, because of the eternal nature of the kingdom, Zephaniah has been used by God to speak specific words of healing into this day for those with diseased organs, brain issues, and mental illness.

The word "mighty" [2] (Hebrew: *gibbor*) describes the might, strength, and power of the King of glory (Psalm 24:8). Continuing through the verse, the word "save" [3] (Hebrew: *yasa*), has within it the underlying thought of bringing to a broad pasture, instead of a narrow strait, symbolic of distress and danger. It further describes the protective duties of a shepherd (Ezekiel 34:22), and conveys the idea of deliverance from tribulation and certain death (Judges 10:13-14; Psalm 22:21).

Rest

As mentioned previously, a homograph is a word with two or more meanings. The word "rest" [6], (Hebrew: *haras*) fits into these criteria. It means to plough and to be silent. Whose back was plowed and remained silent? Of course, it was Jesus! (Isaiah 50:6; 53:7).

When I was saved, we used to sing this verse as a chorus, but the words were changed from, "He will rest in His love" to "We will rest in His love." The truth of the matter, people back then missed the point that this describes the cross. It was Jesus, upon the cross, who was resting in the Father's love. How do I know?

The Hebrew word picture for love (Hebrew: *ahav:* אָהַב), is made up of two components: *av:* אַב Father and *hey:* ה revealed. Together in composition they spell out the heart of the Father revealed. This means that Jesus was resting in His Father's love, and His death upon the cross, *is* the Father revealed.

Finally, the verse is brought to a close with the word "singing." This word [9] (*rinnah*) refers to a shout or cry uttered. May I suggest, in context, this is Jesus' shout of victory from the cross, *"It is finished!"* (John 19:30).

Though he likely had no idea, there really can be no doubt that Zephaniah was prophesying about Christ on the cross. It is unmistakable. Hopefully you made it through the technical stuff to receive the impartation on the revelation this verse contains. What an absolutely power-packed verse!

Application

What part of the verse from Zephaniah spoke the most to you? Why was that?

This is a verse that deserves time in focused meditation. Set aside a portion of your journal to review God's goodness revealed here.

If you or anyone around you need healing in an area described by the provisions hidden in this verse, please take a moment to ask the Holy Spirit to enliven and impart the healing glory concealed here.

Chapter 35

THE AKEDAH

Genesis 22:1-19

One of the clearest parallels of Jesus being offered as a sacrifice on the cross of Calvary is known in Hebrew as the *Akedah*. The word *akedah* (ar-kee-dah) means binding, and is a reference to the binding of Isaac by his father Abraham. This story has been covered before in detail, in my book *The Mystic Awakening*. So, let us quickly establish the validity of the alignment between the two episodes and move to the kingdom provision it releases to us.

The Journey to Mount Moriah

The story began when God asked Abraham to go and offer his son as a burnt offering on a mountain in the land of Moriah. Mount Moriah just happened to be the place identified as the site of Solomon's Temple (2 Chronicles 3:1). After they had set out on their journey, the Bible records, *"On the third day Abraham lifted his eyes and saw the place a far off"* (Genesis 22:4). How long had the son been dead in the father's heart? Answer: three days (Mark 8:31; 9:31; 10:34).

Abraham then directed the young men who have accompanied him to stay at the base of the mount, while he and Isaac ascended to worship (Genesis 22:5). This is the first mention of worship in Scripture. In saying to his servants, *"...I and the lad will go yonder and worship, and come again to you,"* Abraham was also confessing his belief in the resurrection (Genesis 22:5).

Isaac carried the wood on his back up the mount, just as Jesus was made to bear the cross to Golgotha (John 19:17). As they made their way, Isaac asked, *"Where is the lamb for a burnt offering?"* To which Abraham responded, *"God will provide for Himself the lamb for a burnt offering"* (Genesis 22:8).

Having built the altar, Abraham put the wood *"in order"* before *"binding"* his son and placing him upon it (Genesis 22:9). The cross, of course, is wood *prepared* or *put in order*; and *binding*, refers to words or accusations holding a person in preparation for judgment. As Abraham lifted the knife in judgment, God intervened with a substitute, *"behind him was a ram caught in a thicket by his horns"* (Genesis 22:13). The Hebrew word "behind" is also translated "afterward" elsewhere. Afterward, Jesus was offered up as our substitute (John 1:29). The words of accusation were not able to hold Him (Acts 2:24,27). He lay down His authority, strength (horns) (Philippians 2:6-7), wore a crown of thorns (John 19:2), and died in our place (2 Corinthians 5:15).

This episode concluded with, *"So Abraham returned to his young men, and they arose and went..."* (Genesis 22:19). Though Isaac was obviously among them, the Holy Spirit has deliberately omitted to mention him in the returning party so that his nonappearance mirrors Jesus' death upon on the cross. It is pretty conclusive that the two scenes parallel one another.

Remember, Abraham and Isaac physically went through this dramatic scenario. In doing so, because of the eternal nature of the cross, they add dimensional insights not only to Jesus' death, but also reveal promises linked to His vicarious sacrifice.

The Promises

> *And Abraham called the name of that place Jehovah-Jireh: as it is said to this day, In the mount of the Lord it shall be seen* (Genesis 22:14).

This is Abraham speaking as a prophet (Genesis 20:7). Here, there is a double play in the name Jehovah Jireh. The verse itself tells us it means the Lord will see to it, or it shall be seen, which forecasts Christ's coming to that place. The title also means the Lord will provide. The surface prophetic interpretation is of Jesus coming as God's provision. However, what if God is also saying, in seeing Jesus as our sacrifice, there is provision? As in seeing the cross with your inner eye unlocks kingdom provision. Anyway, the story continues:

> *And the angel of the Lord called unto Abraham out of heaven the second time, And said, By myself have I sworn, says the Lord, for because you have done this thing, and have not withheld your son, your only son: That in blessing I will bless you, and in multiplying I will multiply your seed as the stars of the heaven, and as the sand which is upon the sea shore; and your seed shall possess the gate of his enemies; And in your seed shall all the nations of the earth be blessed; because you have obeyed my voice* (Genesis 22:15-18).

The Basis of Multiplication

First up, it is important to recognize that these promises are to Abraham and his offspring. Gentile inclusion is found in recalling the apostle Paul's words, *"those that are of faith, are the children of Abraham"*

(Galatians 3:7; Romans 4:13-16). So what does it mean *"in blessing I will bless you, and in multiplying I will multiply you"*? The key here is to interpret the phrase in context.

The word "bless" (Hebrew: *barak*) used here is derived from the noun "knee." As such, the word suggests a bending or bowing of the knee. Which is in keeping with the thought of obedience found at both the beginning and end of this incident. When Abraham started out, God spoke to him to go and offer his son. At which point, it is recorded that:

> *...Abraham rose up early in the morning, and saddled his donkey, and took two of his young men with him* (Genesis 22:3).

Abraham had hundreds of servants. He took 318 of them with him when he rescued Lot (Genesis 14:14). It was their job to prepare for travel. So when it tells us he saddled his donkey, metaphorically it is saying Abraham harnessed his heart, as a servant. This episode also closed with God's promised blessing because *"you have obeyed My voice."* Therefore, God's promised blessing is couched before and after in obedience. God's blessing is found in the heart of obedience: *"in blessing I will bless you, and in multiplying I will multiply you."*

The degree or cost of Abraham's obedience is what is conveyed in the second part of the promised blessing. This is because the word "multiplying" (Hebrew: *rabah*) speaks of abundance and follows God's recognition of what Abraham had done, *"...because you have done this thing, and have not withheld your son, your only son."*

Abraham gave abundantly in offering up his son; and in return, God responds to this wholehearted obedience with His twofold promised blessing.

Seed

One last thought here is that the word "seed" has many meanings. Abraham's seeds are his offspring, including Christian believers. Abraham's ultimate Seed is Jesus Christ, as the promised Messiah from his generational line. Finally, Abraham's seeds are words of faith (Luke 8:11). Here's the quirky thing, the word "multiplying" also means to shoot an arrow toward its target. Now as words are arrows metaphorically (Psalm 64:3), hidden in this promise is the means to *"possess the gates of His enemies."* If we are wholeheartedly devoted to His cause, the authority of His living word in our mouths will dispossess the enemy's strongholds in and around our lives.

Application

Did you ever see Jesus' death upon the cross as an act of worship?

Have you ever considered worship to be the sacrifice of your life?

From this scene, what do you see as the key to multiplication?

What do you think?

(A) As the offspring of Abraham, are we required to be obedient to see this promise activated?

Or,

(B) Has Christ fully met the conditions required upon Abraham's seed-line?

If you were to come away from the *Akedah* with one thing, what would it be?

Chapter 36

FEEDING THE 5,000

Matthew 14:13-21; Mark 6:30-44;
Luke 9:10-17; John 6:1-14

An Easily Overlooked Verse

There appears to be a random verse in Mark's Gospel that is found, following the disciples' gob-smacking amazement at Jesus walking on the sea. It reads:

> *For they considered not the miracle of the loaves: for their heart was hardened* (Mark 6:52).

This statement says they were amazed beyond measure because they hadn't put the pieces together, that the two miracles—feeding 5,000 and walking on water—were related. So what was the link between the two?

Feeding the People

When Jesus fed the 5,000 men, John's Gospel tells us the Passover was near (John 6:4). Prior to the actual miracle, Jesus was moved with compassion seeing the people because *"they were like sheep without a shepherd,"* and so He started teaching them (Mark 6:34). Then, as it was getting late, His disciples came to Him wanting to disperse the crowds so they could source their own food. At which point, Jesus pressed His disciples to come up with dinner for everyone. After discovering all they had between them was only five loaves and two fish, and confessing 200 denarii of bread would be insufficient to feed them (John 6:7), Jesus takes charge of the situation.

John records that there was much grass in the place (John 6:10). Luke relates that Jesus had them sit in groups of fifty (Luke 9:14); at which point, He took the five loaves and two fish, looked heavenward, blessed, and broke the loaves, and gave the pieces to the disciples to distribute. Jesus then divided the two fish among them all (Mark 6:41). After they had all eaten, Jesus was meticulous in ensuring the leftovers were gathered, from which they filled twelve baskets of the pieces.

Jesus' Ministry to Israel

The feeding of the 5,000 is a picture of Jesus' ministry to Israel. How so, you ask? Five is the number of grace, and a thousand according to Isaiah is the number associated with a clan or nation (Isaiah 60:22). Who is the nation of grace (5 x 1,000)? Answer: Israel. Let's confirm the same, with the elements identified.

Jesus' recognition of the people as *"sheep without a shepherd"* is a display of the heart of God for His people, and a theme throughout Scripture (Numbers 27:17; 1 Kings 22:17; 2 Chronicles 18:16; Matthew 9:36). This is particularly true in regard to poor or corrupt spiritual leadership in Israel. Remember, God was their Shepherd and they His flock (Psalm 80:1; Isaiah 40:11; 63:11; Ezekiel 34:8,11-12; Zechariah 13:7; John 10:2,11). The loaves, being bread, represent the Word of God. There being five loaves means that Jesus did not come with a word of judgment, but one of grace (John 1:14; John 8:11; 12:47; Acts 14:3; 20:32). The breaking of the bread is a picture of Jesus, the Bread of Life (John 6:32), being broken and poured out for Israel.

The two fish represent the witness of revelatory miracles associated with His word (John 8:18; 10:25). Take note here that proportionately the word is to be the mainstay of our diet. Philip's exclamation that 200 denarii would not feed this mob is saying, even if you doubled every-thing the world had to offer, it would not be enough. The grass on which the crowds sat to have their hunger met is the fulfilment of Psalm 23:1-2:

> *The Lord is my shepherd, I shall not want. He makes me to lie down in green pastures.*

The scene is complete by having the people sit in groups of fifty, which means there would be 100 groups (50 x 100 = 5,000). One hundred is representative of the fullness of the flock (Matthew 18:12; Luke 15:4). On the other hand, the time of Passover is mentioned because it links this story with the time of His sacrifice, as the Lamb of God.

Demonstrating Abraham's Promise

Therefore, in looking to heaven and breaking the bread, Jesus is demon-strating the promise given to Abraham at Mount Moriah. He is offering up His life to God to be broken, a substitutionary sacrifice for Israel (John 11:51-52). God's response in multiplying the bread and fish is the fulfilment and confirmation of Abraham's earlier promise.

When Jesus tested His disciples, by asking them to provide for the crowds, He was pressing them to draw from Abraham's promised mul-tiplication. This suggests, that they could, and would, also do the same. As will be seen in the next study.

However, we close this discussion with the disciples required to pick up everything left over, *"Gather up the fragments that remain, that nothing be lost*" (John 6:12). Why was Jesus so insistent that this is done? He did this so that in gathering twelve baskets full of what was left over, there would be a depiction of the infilling of His twelve disciples as He gave Himself to Israel.

Application

Verses of Scripture that get our attention are there so that we will dig deeper and ask questions of the passage. They begin a meditative process that is the avenue for God to release revelation. God wants us to engage with Him—in prayer and in reading our Bibles.

Have any strange or out-of-place Scriptures come to your attention as you have been reading your Bible lately?

In offering up the bread before God and blessing it, Jesus was giving thanks for His Life given in our place. Think about how great is the measure of His love for us!

Jesus deliberately used bread and fish. The bread was His revelatory word, and the fish His revelatory miracles confirming the word. Why do we need both?

This story is a demonstration of the promise given to Abraham. Many people want to see multiplication miracles. What are the requirements?

Chapter 37

WALKING ON WATER

Matthew 14:22-33; Mark 6:45-52; John 6:16-21

For they considered not the miracle of the loaves:
for their heart was hardened (Mark 6:52).

The astonishment of the disciples at Jesus walking on the sea meant they had missed the relevance of His feeding 5,000 people. The fact that this point is raised by Mark indicates that there is more than a sequential connection between the two. Not only does Jesus walking on the sea immediately follow the loaves miracle, there is also a spiritual correlation.

Immediately after the miracle of the loaves, Matthew and Mark tell us Jesus made His disciples get into a ship and go before Him to the other side. John relates why He did so. According to John, Jesus perceived the people would take Him by force and make Him king (John 6:15). So, He averted a preconceived and misguided earthly crowning by dispersing the crowd and sending His disciples ahead to the other side of the lake. It was now night, and Jesus ascended the mount to pray while His disciples were attempting to row across the water. As Jesus was in prayer,

He saw His disciples three or four miles away, toiling in rowing because the wind was against them (Mark 6:48). So He decided to go to them. This is where it gets really interesting.

Different Angles of the Same Scene

Mark reports, that Jesus *"would have passed them by"* had they not freaked out at seeing Him walking on the water (Mark 6:48-51). Matthew tells how Peter stepped out of the boat. He was walking on water by faith until the circumstances around him—the wind and waves—caused doubt to usurp Jesus' command to *"Come."* John, on the other hand, adds that the moment Jesus stepped into the boat, they were at the shore where they had been rowing toward (John 6:21). As Jesus approached them in the fourth watch of the night, all three accounts record that the disciples were afraid because they thought He was a spirit (Matthew 14:26; Mark 6:49; John 6:19). Though their story's capture different angles of the same scene, all three accounts are true and complement one another.

Surprised Disciples

Why were the disciples surprised by His appearing? Mark 6:52 says it was due to a calloused and insensitive heart. They had not understood the previous miracle's significance. With the privilege of hindsight, we understand the miracle of the loaves to be a prophetic enactment of His death for Israel. So the next miracle, following in quick succession, must relate what followed His death. The disciples were to be equally as shocked at His resurrection as they were here in His surprise appearance.

God Is Ever-Watchful

Before Jesus had ascended the mountain to pray and the disciples had set out upon the sea, the crowd wanted to proclaim Him king. The scene echoes the triumphant entry, a lead up to the Passover, where the crowds hailed Him as their awaited Messianic King. Following that feast, Jesus climbing the mount to pray speaks of His ascension. Where He is ever interceding for us (Hebrews 7:25). In seeing the disciples in the darkest hour, the fourth watch, as they struggled to row against contrary winds, this says that He is ever-watchful over us in a world saturated with an opposite spirit.

Four Kingdom Keys

Moses passed through the water; Jesus walked on the water. Moses was symbolically passing through death; whereas, Jesus has overcome death. Jesus now comes to us as the Holy Spirit. Be sensitive; because when He comes, He will pass us by without an invitation into our situation. Just as Peter stepped out on hearing Jesus' command to *"Come,"* we are to do the same when we hear His *rhema* word. Peter teaches us not to let circumstances overpower His word, so that doubt has no place to divide our hearts. When Jesus is aboard, we are there. This means wherever the king is, there is the kingdom with all His provision and glory.

Feeding the 4,000

Matthew 15:32-39; Mark 8:1-10

What about when Jesus subsequently fed 4,000 men? I'm glad you asked that question. Jesus pushed His disciples to provide food at the feeding of the 5,000 for good reason. He believed that they could do the same. The feeding of the 4,000 is a demonstration that they would do the same. In this context, four represents the four corners of the earth (Revelation 7:1). One thousand, as we saw earlier, speaks of a nation. Therefore, four thousand is a picture of the nations of the globe (4 x 1,000 = 4,000). When Jesus fed the 4,000, how many baskets were taken up? The answer is seven (Matthew 15:37). After being broken for Israel,

His disciples would do the same and offer up their lives, like His, to see the hearts (baskets) of the world come to rest (7).

Application

How many times have you read Gospel stories without taking time to consider what kingdom truth is encoded beneath the details?

Jesus may have passed by them but they beckoned Him in by taking time to pray. Do you beckon Him routinely to enter your life situations?

The feeding of the 4,000 is still taking place. What part will you play in seeing the hearts of the world come to rest?

Chapter 38

SOWING TO RECEIVE A HUNDREDFOLD RETURN

Genesis 26:1-33

Isaac lived 180 years, the longest of all the patriarchs, yet less is written about him than the others. Re-digging his father's wells, in Genesis 26, is the only chapter where he is center stage. Given that Gerar is the borderland to the Promised Land, what happens here is pivotal for us as kingdom heirs. Isaac was instructed to *"sojourn"* in the land (Genesis 26:3). However, rather than passing through, he chose to settle down and *"dwell"* (Genesis 26:6). This is Abraham's heir apparent, still clinging to the world around him.

As we read the chapter, it is important to realize that verses 12-15, are an overview of what is about to unfold. Why is this important? Without this understanding, the reader may misconstrue Isaac's sowing and reaping a hundredfold, in a drought, as independent of time and process.

While it does say Isaac sowed and received a hundredfold return in a year, it also says that he *"began to prosper and continued prospering until he became very prosperous"* (Genesis 26:13). This suggests he had to come to a place where he sowed and received his hundredfold return. It takes water to grow seed. At the time of the overview, Isaac hasn't yet dug any wells. By telling us up front he sowed and received his bumper crop, the Holy Spirit wants us to search out and find how from the script.

The Key to Accelerated Growth

Isaac, as heir, is promised a blessing because of the obedience of his father (Genesis 26:3-5). We are in a similar position, having arrived as heirs by faith in the obedience of Jesus (Romans 4:13-14; Hebrews 5:8; James 2:5). This means that like Isaac, we are invited into accelerated growth to become mature sons and daughters by following the outline of this passage (John 1:12). Isaac had been there *"a long time"* as an heir (Genesis 26:8). When something happened, that accelerated his development, marked by his progression through the wells. He was initially pushed out of his comfort zone by Abimelech, who confronted him about a lie (Genesis 26:8-10,16). Isaac was then propelled by his family's physical need, a famine, and repeated opposition to search out new wells. The key to his spiritual growth is found in the onward journey through the wells.

Isaac and Abimelech

Isaac's connection with Abimelech is a metaphor of his relationship with God. Abimelech means father of the king. When Abimelech confronted him about saying Rebekah was his sister rather than his wife, it is a picture of God addressing the disharmony between Isaac's head and his heart (1 Corinthians 11:7; Psalm 16:9). In the story, Abimelech says to Isaac, *"Go from us, because you are mightier than we"* (Genesis 26:16). The word "mighty" has a double meaning. It does mean many, but it also means to close or cover the eyes. So while Abimelech was addressing a potential threat, God was revealing to Isaac that his spirit, his inner eye, was covered. Leaving Abimelech's country meant that where he had once been comfortable in being supplied water, he was now forced to dig for his own.

The Wells

Esek

The first well, Esek, is named after the events surrounding its discovery. Its name means contention. It depicts a claim and counterclaim tug-of-war over the appearance of the life-giving water of revelation. The narrative reports that the Philistines had stopped and filled the wells with earth (Genesis 26:15,18). This is a picture of spiritual forces blocking the flow with earthly thoughts. Esek depicts a believer searching for words of revelation, but natural cares are crowding out and smothering the word.

Sitnah

The roots of the word Sitnah carry the thought of legal accusation. Once an heir shakes free of the world and gets a taste of what he or she is entitled to, the enemy comes to challenge its legality. Isaac's opposition at Sitnah depicts religious spirits trying to regulate and control an heir's access to revelation. Jesus met this type of resistance when the Pharisees confronted Him about the source of His authority.

Rehoboth

This was the first place where there was no opposition. It was here that Isaac discovered room to move and recognized his potential fruitfulness.

> *And he removed from there, and dug another well, and for that they strove not: and he called the name of it Rehoboth; and he said, For now the Lord has made room for us, and we shall be fruitful in the land* (Genesis 26:22).

Rehoboth carries the thought of roomy or spaciousness. The Hebrew word "roomy" literally means the man of the inner chamber. Therefore, the journey to Rehoboth is the discovery that *"the kingdom of God is within you"* (Luke 17:21). When believers discover the kingdom, they are brought into a broad land where there are no limits. For Isaac, Rehoboth was the entry point to go higher. It was Rehoboth that took him to another level, because the text records that his next move was *up* to Beersheba (Genesis 26:23). Discovering the reality of the kingdom hidden in plain sight opens the heart to greater devotion.

Beersheba

At Beersheba, the Scriptures note that Isaac built his first altar and pitched his tent. The altar speaks of him laying his life down before God. The tent refers to a new desire for God's presence. In going *up* to Beersheba, Isaac is entering the eternal realm. Here, he personally encountered God. Here, he came into the very Council of God. His covenant and witness with Abimelech was but an earthly shadow of what had previously taken place. In calling the place Beersheba, we are privy to understand that he not only made a covenant with Abimelech but with God. Beersheba means Well of the Oath and Well of the Seven. The dual meaning tells us he also entered the throne room of God. This is because, the seven being spoken of here are seven ewe lambs that Abraham previously gave to Abimelech, when he too cut a covenant with him (Genesis 21:27-31). Why did Abraham give Abimelech seven ewe lambs? He was reflecting on earth, what he also had seen in heaven. The seven ewe lambs represented the *"seven Spirits of God"* that go throughout the earth (Zechariah 4:10; Revelation 5:6).

That which had been a personal and intimate encounter with God for Isaac remains hidden. Yet, it is subtly portrayed through his meeting with Abimelech, Phichol, and Ahuzzath, for those with eyes to see. Abimelech means father of the king. Phichol is described as commander of the army, and Ahuzzath is recorded as a friend, adviser, or support in trial. Therefore, the Scriptures are reflecting Isaac's entrance before the heavenly Council of God.

Isaac's covenant with Abimelech also marks his deeper connection with God. He is no longer living in his father's shadow but has stepped into his own encounter with God. His arrival at Beersheba marks those who are no longer heirs apparent, but have now become sons.

Having discovered the breadth of the kingdom at Rehoboth, in moving to Beersheba, Isaac laid down his life and gave his all before God. How was it that Isaac sowed and received a hundredfold return in the same year? It was here, at Beersheba, that he activated the promise given to his father Abraham: *"In blessing, I will bless you, in multiplying, I will multiply you...."*

Isaac's journey to Beersheba is incredibly important for heirs transitioning to sonship. It provides hope in seeing the big picture so that we are not overwhelmed and do not get lost along the way. Second, God knows we want to access more of the kingdom, but He also wants us to grow up so that He can entrust us with more.

Application

At what stage along the way would you see yourself in Isaac's journey to kinship?

A. Discomforted

B. Esek: Facing contention

C. Sitnah: Facing religious challenges

D. Rehoboth: Recognizing the kingdom within

E. Beersheba: Laying your life down that He might live through you

Do you think it is helpful to see the big picture? Why?

If a lie is disharmony between the head and the heart, what is truth?

Has the discovery of the kingdom hidden in plain sight caused you to adore and pursue Him more?

Pray that God would take you deeper into an encounter before His throne.

Chapter 39

ISAIAH

Prophetically Contextualizing Unbelief

Though Jesus performed so many miracles, the people's response was staggering—*"they did not believe in Him"* (John 12:37). On one occasion, the apostle John quoted from the prophet Isaiah to prophetically contextualize what was going on. John 12:37-41 (NKJV) says:

> But although He had done so many signs before them, they did not believe in Him, that the word of Isaiah the prophet might be fulfilled, which he spoke: "Lord, who has believed our report? And to whom has the arm of the Lord been revealed?" Therefore they could not believe, because Isaiah said again: "He has blinded their eyes and hardened their hearts, lest they should see with their eyes, lest they should understand with their hearts and turn, So that I should heal them." These things Isaiah said when he saw His glory and spoke of Him.

An Eternal Perspective

In quoting from Isaiah, John freely drew from the prophet's writings out of the order in which they were written. John referenced the 53rd chapter in the Book of Isaiah before the 6th, linking the two passages from an eternal perspective. It is important to realize that both were an existent reality before the cross had physically taken place. John relates it was at Isaiah's throne room encounter that the Lord spoke of the people's blindness and hardened hearts. The passage is a window revealing a glimpse of the majesty of the Lord Jesus Christ.

Isaiah Chapter Six

Here's the amazing thing, hidden in the first verse of that chapter is Isaiah 53! The opening line of the chapter reads, *"In the year that King Uzziah died, I saw also the Lord sitting..."* (Isaiah 6:1). Before pride entered his heart, Uzziah was a godly king. A record of Uzziah's achievements is found in Second Chronicles 26:1-23. There is a parallel between Jesus and Uzziah. Uzziah's name means strength of the Lord. In speaking of Jesus, the apostle John quoted, *"to whom has the arm of the Lord been revealed?"* (Isaiah 53:1).

In Scripture, the arm is a symbol of strength. Jesus was God's arm, His strength revealed. The king was recognized for successfully warring against the Philistines. Jesus went about *"healing all who were oppressed by the devil"* (Acts 10:38). Uzziah built towers in Jerusalem. Jesus made Peter, James, and John into pillars (Galatians 2:9). Uzziah led an army of more than 300,000 men; Jesus is the Lord of hosts (Psalm 24:10). Uzziah loved farming, Jesus is the Chief Shepherd (1 Peter 5:4), and His Father the husbandman (John 15:1). Alas, Uzziah died a leper, smitten of God. Jesus became sin and was struck by God (2 Corinthians 5:21; Zechariah 13:7).

How did Uzziah become a leper? He was struck with leprosy because of pride; he usurped his public office by attempting to burn incense in the temple. The root of humanity's sin is found in the devil's pride and attempt to ascend in heaven (Isaiah 14:12-13). Therefore, King Uzziah's life and death is a metaphor of Jesus. Hidden in Isaiah chapter 6 is the cross, preceding Isaiah's glimpse of the King on His heavenly throne.

The Cross in the Throne Room

Furthermore, the cross is hidden in the actual throne room scene. When confronted with God's holiness, Isaiah is undone and immediately confessed the sin of his lips. The passage reads:

> *Then said I, Woe is me! for I am undone; because I am a man of unclean lips, and I dwell in the midst of a people of unclean lips: for my eyes have seen—the King, the Lord of hosts. Then flew one of the seraphim unto me, having a live coal in his hand, which he had taken with the tongs from off the altar: And he laid it upon my mouth, and said, Lo, this has touched your lips; and your iniquity is taken away, and your sin purged* (Isaiah 6:5-7).

What was it that was placed on his lips to purge Isaiah of his sin? It was a live coal from the altar. What is it that makes atonement for sin? It is the blood of an offering (Exodus 30:10; Leviticus 17:11). Did you notice that the coal was still hot? That's what makes it a live coal. It is still glowing from the sacrifice it consumed and the blood it received. This means in heaven there is an altar before God that received the precious blood of Christ, and it is ever hot (Revelation 13:8). This passage from Isaiah, who lived 700 years before Christ, is proof of the eternal coexistence of cross and kingdom. No wonder the apostle John had the liberty to freely quote Isaiah without consideration of his time of writing.

The Seraphim

Above it stood the seraphim: each one had six wings with two he covered his face, and with two he covered his feet, and with two he did fly (Isaiah 6:2).

The angels described in the throne room had six wings. In that, two covered his face, two covered his feet, and with two he flew, we discover the priority of heaven's workforce. The angels of God spend two-thirds of their time in worship and one-third in working. As we draw to a close in this series of studies, I believe we are encouraged to do the same, that earth would mirror heaven.

Shelve or Share?

Also I heard the voice of the Lord, saying, Whom shall I send, and who will go for us? Then said I, Here am I; send me (Isaiah 6:8).

Like Isaiah, our exposure beyond the cross to the King and His kingdom requires a response from us. Will we shelve or share the reality of the kingdom hidden beyond plain sight?

Healing Revival

And he said, Go, and tell this people, Hear you indeed, but understand not; and see you indeed, but perceive not. Make the heart of this people fat, and make their ears heavy, and shut their eyes; lest they see with their eyes, and hear with their ears, and understand with their heart, and convert, and be healed (Isaiah 6:9-10).

What is inferred by this passage is that this release of fresh revelation says we are poised for an outpouring of healing. As eyes and ears are being opened and the insulating fat of religious understanding is removed, hearts will begin to burn with new zeal. This is the knowledge of the glory of God that is to fill the whole earth—and a healing revival will witness to its message.

Application

In relation to time, the kingdom of heaven has an eternal perspective. What does that mean to you?

Isaiah did not have his throne room encounter until King Uzziah had passed over. What do you think could be the reason for this?

The cross has always been in the throne room of God. Answer one of the following:

1. What are some of the implications of this?

2. Why do you think this is so?

If two-thirds of your time was given to worship, what would that look like for you?

What could you do to strengthen your ability to share the kingdom hidden in plain sight?

We tend to think of divine healing as a sovereign, independent act. However, God inferred that closed eyes and ears and dull hearts hold back healing. So, what needs to accompany a sustained healing revival?

Chapter 40

PSALM 133

Brethren Dwelling Together

Behold, how good and how pleasant it is for brethren to dwell together in unity! It is like the precious ointment upon the head, that ran down upon the beard, even Aaron's beard: that went down to the skirts of his garments; As the dew of Hermon, and as the dew that descended upon the mountains of Zion: for there the Lord commanded—the blessing, even life forevermore (Psalm 133:1-3).

Breaking Free of Preconceived Notions

One of the major issues we have when we are reading a familiar passage of Scripture, like Psalm 133, is the conditioned and preconceived notions that are resident in our hearts. If this were taught to you as a call for corporate unity in the church or home, then it is likely that's how you will continue to look at it.

However, remember *every Old Testament promise has its ultimate fulfillment in Christ*. So, let us look at this psalm in the light of the cross. From that perspective, the first and last lines reveal that a certain type of unity leads to eternal life. Life forevermore is equivalent to eternal life. What type of unity leads to eternal life? Now, knowing the Holy Spirit teaches comparing spiritual things with spiritual (1 Corinthians 2:13), if we recall, Jesus is not ashamed to call us brothers and sisters (Hebrews 2:11) and insert that here. What we see is that unity with Jesus releases the blessing of eternal life. That makes sense, in the light of the cross, doesn't it?

An Anointed High Priest

The middle two metaphors in Psalm 133 confirm this conclusion. The first of these describes the goodness and pleasantness, as like the consecration of Aaron, the high priest (Exodus 29:7; Leviticus 8:12). In light of the cross, who is our High Priest? He is no other but Jesus Christ. Aaron was anointed upon the head to consecrate him to the priesthood. He was sanctified. That is, he was removed from the profane and empowered to operate in the realm of the sacred. That brings new insight into Jesus' comments at Bethany, when He said, *"...she has poured this ointment on my body, she did it for my burial"* (Matthew 26:12). This was an anointing to set Him apart as our High Priest, as He was about to enter the Most Holy Place in heaven. We know from John's Gospel that Mary wiped His feet with her hair (John 12:3), so like the psalm, the anointing oil flowed down to the skirts of His garments.

The anointing oil used in the tabernacle was not used for any other purpose. Given its specific formulation (Exodus 30:23-25) means that when the high priest was anointed, it released a fragrance he never forgot. You could say that pleasant aroma was carried with him wherever he went. It should not surprise us when His presence is signaled by a beautiful fragrance in our meetings. As fragrances may be associated with aspects of His character, the presence also signals that aspect in operation. He will come to meet a need. For example, a honey aroma may relate revelation is being released, a lavender fragrance may indicate the spirit of understanding is in operation, and the odor of smoke may indicate the glory of His consuming fire is present.

When an earthly high priest would make atonement, it would cover Israel's sin for a year. Our heavenly High Priest who offered His own sinless blood to God not only covered our sin but cleansed our conscience as well (Hebrews 9:14). Therefore, His union with us means no one can condemn us (Romans 8:1). We are denying the power of His blood if we condemn ourselves. On a relational footing, our union means each of us now has an Intercessor in heaven. What assurance that brings! He is ever available to bring us to complete salvation when we turn to Him (Hebrews 7:25).

The Dew of Heaven

Our union with Him is also described *"as the dew of Hermon and as the dew that descended upon the mountains of Zion"* (Psalm 133:3). As an introduction to understanding the significance and meaning of this metaphor, consider Gideon's fleece before God. The Bible says:

> *And Gideon said unto God, If You will save Israel by my hand, as You have said, Behold, I will put a fleece of wool in the floor; and if the dew be on the fleece only, and it be dry upon all the earth beside, then shall I know that You will save Israel by my hand, as You have said. And it was so: for he rose up early on the morrow, and thrust the fleece together, and wrung the dew out of the fleece, a bowl full of water. And Gideon said unto God, Let not Your anger be hot against me and I will speak but this once: let me prove, I pray You, but this once with the fleece; let it now be dry only upon the fleece, and upon all the ground let there be dew.' And God did so that night: for it was dry*

upon the fleece only, and there was dew on all the ground (Judges 6:36-40).

So, the first night the dew fell on the fleece, and the second night it fell on the ground. Remember, this was a confirmation that God would save Israel through Gideon's leadership. The fleece represented the Lamb of God—Jesus Christ. When the dew fell on the fleece, it indicated the favor of God upon Christ as He ministered as a living Sacrifice under an open heaven. It means God's acceptance of the Lamb slain for the sins of the world. The ground is humanity, outside of Christ (2 Corinthians 4:7).

The second night, things have changed. Now, heaven has been opened and the favor of God could once again fall upon humankind. God displayed an eternal truth to confirm His warrior's selection. Because of the cross, He is with us, and you and I walk under an open heaven. As a son or daughter, like Gideon, you are also anointed to lead.

The manna in the wilderness came with the dew (Numbers 11:9). Thus, the blessing of our union brings with it the distillation of pure revelation. God's speech is as subtle as dew (Deuteronomy 32:2). When Isaac blessed his two sons, the order in which he spoke of the dew communicated the priority and authority of the spirit realm over the natural (Genesis 27:28,39). This is a reminder to make decrees, overwriting the natural order of things, based on your own revelation or the material you have found in this volume.

As we have found throughout, coming from the heavens, dew is multidimensional (Zechariah 8:12). Finally, as dew is lost in the heat of the day, don't find yourself so busy that you don't take time to sit with Him, especially early (Exodus 16:14; Hosea 6:4). As you do so, learn to meditate on the Scriptures, because dew gathers in intimacy and contemplation (Proverbs 3:19-20).

Final Thoughts

You may be disappointed that there has to be a final chapter. If the Lord so willed it, we could go on, opening up narrative after narrative from both the Old Testament and Gospels. However, the examples that have been covered present enough material, with confirmatory Scripture, to affirm the concepts that have been set forth as doctrinally sound. At the same time, I believe God was in the subject selection process to ensure a good foundation of key kingdom principles and insights was covered. This has by no means been an exhaustive study—there are hundreds of other narratives, psalms, and prophetic passages that were not covered. Basically, this was an orientation process, to build confidence, so that every reader would be empowered to step out on their own journey of discovery.

Jesus was with the disciples for forty days unveiling the kingdom to them. He didn't teach everything they needed to know at that time. After He had ascended, their conditioning and bias meant they were even blind, for a while, to the Gentiles being engrafted. Instead of downloading everything at once, He sent the Holy Spirit to lead and empower them the rest of the way. Invite Him now to take you further into other realms of His kingdom.

Application

This book has barely scratched the surface in opening the kingdom hidden within the Scriptures—there are more narratives and verses God wants to open to you. Go back over some of the stories we have explored or visit others of interest to you and continue to explore His magnificent kingdom.

ABOUT THE AUTHOR

Adrian Beale has an ability to release the Spirit of Understanding so that individuals and congregations are awakened and enlivened to new levels of revelation. He loves to open Old Covenant passages to bring out relevant kingdom truth and also interpret the voice of the Spirit in dreams, visions, and supernatural phenomena while cementing his audiences on the Word of God. He has ministered extensively in the USA, Canada, New Zealand, and Australia. He is the co-author of the bestselling book, *The Divinity Code to Understanding your Dreams and Visions* and author of *The Mystic Awakening* and *The Lost Kingdom*.

Adrian can be reached on the web at:
www.everrestministries.com

Follow him on Facebook and Instagram:
@adrianbeale

Experience a personal revival!

Spirit-empowered content from today's top Christian authors delivered directly to your inbox.

Join today!
lovetoreadclub.com

Inspiring Articles
Powerful Video Teaching
Resources for Revival

Get all of this and so much more, e-mailed to you twice weekly!

LOVE TO READ CLUB

by **D DESTINY IMAGE**

CPSIA information can be obtained
at www.ICGtesting.com
Printed in the USA
LVHW080852121119
636958LV00011B/279/P